ACTING

AND HOW TO BE GOOD AT IT

THE SECOND EDITION

ACTING

and how to be
good at it

BASIL HOFFMAN

with a foreword by Sydney Pollack

THE SECOND EDITION

Ingenuity Press USA

First edition copyright © 2006 by Basil Hoffman
Second edition copyright © 2008 by Basil Hoffman

Library of Congress Control Number 2008932347
ISBN 978-0-9715410-2-3

Design by Gopa & Ted2, Inc.
Printed in the United States of America

DEDICATION

CHRISTINE, to whom I was married for more than 17 years, was an indispensable partner to me in every aspect of my life. Her love, her unwavering support, her gentle (but always honest) criticism, the high standards she set for herself, and her grace (and beauty) enriched me personally and professionally in many, many ways, and I am very grateful. Her unfailingly joyous, uplifting encouragement (and, often, financial help) to others, even at times of her own sometimes extreme personal difficulty, was a wonder to behold. She was the most selfless and courageous person I have ever known.

Besides Christine's indescribable positive impact on my life in general, her keen sense of truthfulness and good taste kept me on track every step of the way in the creation of this (and my previous) volume. Without her influence, neither book would have been written.

My gratitude to Christine is greater than I ever told her and greater than I can express here. Nevertheless, I am dedicating *Acting and How to Be Good at It* to her memory as my best attempt at sufficient thanks.

I will never forget.

CONTENTS

FOREWORD xv

TWO CONVERSATIONS xvii

PREFACE xix

I. INTRODUCTION 1

II. PROFESSIONAL ACTING 5

How do you define professionalism?   5

What is acting?   8

Is acting a craft or an art?   9

Should acting be like real life?   10

What is "Amplified Realism"?   10

Is film (camera) acting different from stage acting?   11

What is slick acting?   12

What is autobiographical acting?   12

What are the differences between audition, rehearsal
and performance acting?   14

Is classical acting different from acting in more
contemporary works?   15

What is "at-oneness"?   16

How important is imagination in acting?   17

Are there special techniques for playing comedy?   18

III. DECISIONS ON TRAINING 19

What are the most important attributes for someone
who wants an acting career?   19

Why is training necessary? 20

What do my goals have to do with my training choices? 20

Where should I go to study? 21

How do I find a good school or teacher? 22

Can an actor be permanently harmed by destructive
teachers and teaching methods? 24

Should I accept acting jobs before I finish my training? 25

What is the difference between teaching and coaching,
and are teachers and coaches the same people? 26

Should I lose my accent? 27

IV. Approaches to Training 31

What is the fallacy of scene study? 32

What is the value of improvisation? 33

What is "monologue power"? 33

V. Character Study 37

What is "Subjective Situation Perception," and why do
I need to know about it? 38

How does an actor begin work on a role? 42

What are stage directions and narrative, and are they
important to an actor's performance? 43

What is a character's "essence," and why is it important
for me to identify it? 44

Does the character's essence contain elements of the
actor's essence? 45

What is the difference between playing an attitude
and playing a character, and are attitude and essence
the same thing? 47

What constitutes the physicality of a character? 47

What does "living in the moment" mean, and what is
its importance? 48

Why are the differences between "what" and "how"
so important?   49

What are "inner cues"?   50

What is "privileged information"?   51

What do you mean by "natural sequence of behavior"?   53

Is there a difference between demonstrating and
indicating?   54

What does "permission" have to do with acting?   55

How important is the element of surprise, and how
can I get that into my performance?   56

What is memory of emotion, and what does it have
to do with the actor's "comfort zone"?   57

Is there some technical way to express the meanings
of the words?   61

What is subtext?   64

What is the "point" of a line of dialogue?   65

What is a "thought pause"?   67

What is "vocality" of character?   70

What do you mean when you say, "Forget the words"?   73

What is phrasing?   73

What is grouping?   74

What is a beat?   75

What are obstacles and what is their importance?   76

Can you explain the meaning and the importance
of conflict?   78

What is "programmed behavior"?   78

What is the "tone" of a script, and how should that
affect my approach to the work?   79

What is the difference between naturalism and
truthfulness?   80

When you discuss "purpose," do you really mean
"objective"?   81

What does reporting have to do with acting?   83

Why is listening so important? Is there some
special way to listen?   84

What does the word "compass" mean when you
use it in discussing a role or performance?   85

Do you recommend any specific acting exercises?   85

VI. GETTING THE JOBS 101

What is "actor's conceit," and why is it important?   103

What are the two fundamental truths about every
script?   103

What is type casting, and how does it affect an actor's
employability?   105

How do I approach the part if there are only a few
lines of dialogue?   106

Is there a special way to approach homework?   106

Isn't the concept of "getting it fast" necessarily
superficial, and why is it so difficult for actors to be
truthful with only a small amount of preparation?   108

How do you characterize the relationship between
the actor and the writer?   109

What are "Cornerstones of Truth"?   112

How will I know if I should use an accent or dialect?   113

VII. DOING THE JOB 117

How important is an actor's attitude in the workplace,
and what constitutes a positive attitude?   117

Will I always be given a complete script?   120

Should I approach every script in the same way,
and are there guidelines to follow?   121

What do you mean when you say, "Break down
the script to energize it"?   122

Do I need to memorize the part word for word?   124

When is it appropriate to ask questions about
the work, and how do I know whom to ask?   127

In film and television, does an actor have to give
the same performance in every take?   128

Will the director direct me?   130

Will the director direct me before I begin to act?   132

What does a director mean when he says, "Make it
bigger"?   134

What does a director mean when he says, "Bring it
down" or "It's over the top"?   136

If I'm directed to do the scene faster or slower or
bigger or smaller or louder or quieter, how can I
make that quick adjustment without being artificial?   137

What is a line reading, and what purpose does it serve? 138

What is a "thought reading"?   139

Will the director ever direct me in a language I don't
understand, and is there a reliable way to deal with
that situation?   139

Is the stage director always in charge of final
creative decisions?   140

Is the movie director always in charge of final
creative decisions?   141

Is the television director always in charge of final
creative decisions?   141

What should I do if the other actors aren't good,
are unprepared or misbehave in some way?   142

Does the process of discovery end with homework?   143

How do you work on a part you have been hired
to play but didn't audition for?   143

What is "collaborative cooperation"?   145

When do actors have to do their own makeup?   145

How much input is an actor allowed to have when it
comes to things like props and wardrobe?   146

Should the actor deal directly with the cinematographer,
and how can that affect his performance?   150

What effect does the film editor have on an actor's
performance, and does the actor have direct contact
with the editor?   151

What is A.D.R.?   153

How do you deal with being fired?   153

VIII. COMMERCIALS 155

How do actors get auditions for commercials?   157

Do commercials make demands on the actor that are
different from the demands of stage and screen work?   158

IX. CAREER MANAGEMENT 161

What necessities should an actor acquire
as he pursues a career?   162

What is "thinking in the profession"?   162

Are there any guidelines for starting and maintaining
an acting career?   163

What are actors' most serious career mistakes?   164

What do star actors have in common?   166

Doesn't luck play some part in an actor's success?   167

Can one negative professional experience damage my
career?   169

Are there any special industry information sources
that I should know about?   170

X. CONCLUSION 173

ACKNOWLEDGEMENTS 175

INDEX 185

FOREWORD ⦚

BASIL HOFFMAN writes about acting from the inside of the craft in a practical, clear way, without mumbo-jumbo or mystique. He knows what he's writing about, and you can feel his years of experience on the pages of this book.

—Sydney Pollack

Author's note:

Sydney Pollack died on May 26, 2008. He was a true gentleman, in every sense. Beyond being enriched by having worked with Sydney, I came away from every encounter and every conversation I had with him feeling that I was special in some way. And it started on my first day on location for *The Electric Horseman*, before I shot a single scene, when I received a bottle of Chivas Regal with a note that read, "Basil – Welcome. Sydney." As great a man and as busy as he was, Sydney was always accessible and gracious. His generous foreword for this book is a typical example. He must have known how important his words of praise for my book would be to me. I will always be grateful for the opportunity I was given to work with him. I will never forget his kindness and his generosity. He has left a legacy of great integrity and humanity, as an artist and as a person. I am sad that he is gone.

Basil Hoffman
August 1, 2008

TWO CONVERSATIONS ▪

A Conversation
(a play)

Character: This is so sad. This is the saddest day of my life. This is the saddest moment of my life. I feel like crying. I am going to cry.

Actor: No! I don't think this is so sad. I don't feel like crying. I don't want to cry. I'm not going to cry.

Character: Nobody cares what you think. Nobody cares what you want. Nobody cares how you feel. The audience won't pay money to come into the theatre to find out how you feel. It is not your job to tell the audience what you think. It is not your job to tell the audience what you want. It is your job to do what I tell you to do.

Another Conversation
(another play)

Character: I want to know everything. Tell me everything.

Actor: I can't tell you everything. Some of it is privileged information.

Character: But what if it's important?

Actor: If it's important for you to know it, you'll know it when it happens.

Beirut, Lebanon
February 2002

PREFACE ∷

MY TWO VERY SHORT PLAYS, *A Conversation* and *Another Conversation*, were written during the first week of an acting workshop I conducted for third-year film students at the Academie Libanaise des Beaux-Arts (ALBA) in Beirut, Lebanon, in February 2002. I wrote the plays to explain and clarify, as simply and directly as possible, some important aspects of the acting process. It was a response to the students' confusion caused by years of reading and hearing academic (theoretical and impractical) notions about acting, particularly the relationship of actor to character.

I am indebted to my friend Habib Fadel, a Lebanese actor whom I coached and taught for several months in Los Angeles, for his suggestion that I teach in Lebanon and for his introduction to Khalil Smayra, who invited me to Beirut and who entrusted his students at ALBA to my direct (non-psychological and non-mechanical) approach to the teaching of acting.

The workshop was successful, even beyond my most optimistic expectations. At the end of my first week, I was summoned to Khalil's office and was confronted by folded arms and a silent, inscrutable stare that lasted for the better part of a minute. Finally, Khalil spoke. "You make my students cry." Then he grinned. Every one of the fifteen students in the class had reported to him that for the first time real feelings had come out of them in their work, not their own inappropriate or painful feelings, but the character's feelings.

Even teaching them in their third language (Arabic and French are dual first languages for most of them), I was able to communicate the simplicity of an unconditionally truthful idea of acting. I am grateful to the students in that class for the risks they took in accepting the newness (to them) of this approach. Their achievements in that short period of time reinforced my conviction that truthful acting is a universal concept, easily understandable and readily available to any actor, of any age or nationality, willing to submit to it. Complete truthfulness is the ideal, sometimes elusive, but it must be the goal. For me, as an actor and a teacher (and an audience member), there is no other way.

I. INTRODUCTION

IN MY FIRST BOOK, *Cold Reading and How to Be Good at It,* published in 1998, my intention was to provide a useful tool for professional actors who believe their auditioning skills are not equal to the demands of the auditioning process, particularly as it relates to preparing new material in a limited amount of time.

Since that time, it has become increasingly clear to me that many actors view the audition process as something apart from acting, as if it were possible to achieve some degree of mastery of one without the other. It isn't possible. For that reason, I have written this book as a belated, but necessary, prelude to my book on cold reading.

The intended audience for this book is every actor who aspires to have a professional career and every actor who believes that some important aspect of his concept of craft and career needs a different or more specific and more practical approach. Of course, this also applies to the actor who has a desire to improve his abilities in order to pursue a non-professional acting avocation. In any event, the actor should aspire to the highest standard of excellence that he can attain.

My own personal experiences and observations as a professional actor are the only basis for the contents of this book. The only references I make to systems, methods, techniques, styles or disciplines of other acting teachers and theorists, past and present, are for the purpose of explaining why some particular concepts (and definitions) have been unsatisfactory to me.

The format I have chosen for this book, as I did for the previous book, is in the form of questions and answers. As before, most of the questions were asked by actors in my workshops, seminars, classes and private teaching and coaching sessions. Some of the questions are those that should have been asked but weren't.

As I did in my earlier volume, when referring to any non-specific person, I use the words "he," "him" and "his" in the context of the dictionary definition, "one whose sex is unknown or immaterial." No other words would be both grammatical and all-inclusive.

Every worthwhile acting concept should be applicable to all stages of the acting experience, from the first day of homework to the final performance. With that in mind, it has been unavoidable for me to repeat some ideas throughout the book, wherever it seems important for those points to be revisited. In instances in which a question might be appropriately included in several sections of the book, I have chosen to place it where I believe the actor's work process most needs to have the question answered.

Actors who have read my first book will find that some of the subjects addressed in that book also appear in this book, but that the material is covered somewhat differently. In some cases, I have made changes for purposes of achieving greater clarity. In other instances, the changes are for the purpose of training the actor in the improvement of his craft instead of fulfilling the necessities of cold reading preparation.

The portions of this book related specifically to the profession (as opposed to the craft) of acting are not intended to be a comprehensive guide to the acting business. I have included those references and one separate career management section of the book only to highlight the necessity of a serious businesslike approach to professional acting. The acting I do, the acting I teach and the acting I write about is not theoretical. It is serious *business*.

I have been blessed with experiences in the acting profession that have given me invaluable insights into the reasons why some things work and others don't. Most of what I have learned, I learned by acting (sometimes successfully, sometimes not so successfully), and much of it I have learned from interacting with and observing actors and directors (and others) whose careers have given them the authority to offer or demonstrate ideas that I regard as important. In many instances, I was a most fortunate participant or first-hand observer.

My experiences and my associations in this business have been invaluable to my craft and career, and I feel the need to pass on as much of it as I can. I know that readers of this book (non-actors as well as actors) will profit from those experiences as I have, at the very least by gaining an understanding and appreciation of acting and of the professional acting experience.

II. PROFESSIONAL ACTING ⦂

THE ACTING I WRITE ABOUT in this book has tangible goals attached to it. It is neither academic nor theoretical. It is not class-room acting. It doesn't seek a diploma for successful completion of the course, nor does it long for the approval of a teacher or praise from classmates. This is the acting that produces jobs, careers and money. Sometimes a lot of money.

The defining difference between classroom acting and professional acting is the minimum standard demanded of the actor. Professional acting, particularly in Los Angeles and New York, has the highest stan-dards. The best, most successful actors (and directors) in the world are attracted to this country by the allure of greater fame, more money and the freest society on earth, not to mention the prospect of working with other highly skilled artists at the top of their profession.

Hundreds of high school and college classroom award-winning actors come to Los Angeles and New York every year, believing that they have attained that necessary standard. Most of them have not. The acting profession neither requires nor respects diplomas. But it demands, at the very least, a professional level of proficiency. This book provides some means for recognizing and attaining a high stan-dard of professional acting.

■ *How do you define professionalism?*

I define professionalism according to its *minimum* requirements. The acting profession makes only four demands. These four essential elements of professionalism are: promptness, preparedness, propriety and principle. For an actor, this boils down to being on time, knowing your lines, behaving yourself and being trustworthy. Merely meeting those demands, however, won't ensure any degree of success. Conversely, noncompliance with *any one* of these four prerequisites will invite failure, unless you have become such a big star that they just have to have you, no matter what. Otherwise, don't push your luck.

Promptness is the first indicator of reliability. Are you dependable? They need to know that you will be there when they need you. Tardiness doesn't inspire confidence. There are also personal and emotional aspects to promptness. Your ability or inability to be prompt will have an impact on the emotional response, positive or negative, that you engender in business situations in which you are *needed* to be on time. Nobody you will ever meet in the business is unimportant enough to be kept waiting. As a practical matter, your being late will cost them money, which is not a good thing. On the job, an actor should consider being *more* than prompt. On a personal note, I arrive at the theatre, studio or location hours before I am needed. When the job is a feature film, I go to work one day early (without pay). The purpose is to become familiar with my own working environment, the personalities, the director's methods, and, most importantly, with the character's living and working environment.

Preparedness indicates a good work ethic and a reliable actor. Knowing your lines on the job is a good place to start. There is no remedy for the pervasive sinking feeling that infects *everybody* on a set when an actor struggles fruitlessly to remember his lines.

Propriety means appropriateness, in every sense. It means speaking appropriately, dressing appropriately and behaving appropriately in all situations. If you are compulsively prone to inappropriate speech, attire or behavior, get over it now. Attending a "black tie" event in an open-necked shirt won't create the impression you hope for. Instead of reaping admiration for your creative individualism, you will be correctly perceived as self-centered and foolish. Good behavior is an asset. Invest in it.

Principle is a word that encompasses all aspects of exemplary character. That includes honesty, uprightness, decency, morality and truth-telling. In my previous volume, *Cold Reading and How to Be Good at It*, I omitted this aspect of professionalism because it is such a basic ingredient of civilized behavior that I assumed it to be taken for granted. I have included it here because, unfortunately, the level of public discourse has become so debased that people have begun to expect, and even accept, slipshod morality, especially in those whose positions used to command respect. *Don't lower your standards.* Trust your own highest instincts to lead you personally and professionally. You will be rewarded for it. In practicality, this industry *depends* upon the highest level of morality in all aspects of the business of the business. Million-dollar deals are consummated every day by telephone, *with the written record delivered after the fact*. In my own experience, *only one* prospective employer (out of hundreds of professional jobs) ever failed to live up to the verbal deal. Few other businesses could be so successfully conducted only on the basis of spoken agreements.

The best examples of admirable professional behavior can frequently be found at the top of the profession. Star actors, for whom every job carries enormous responsibility and pressure, are the most prepared, most cooperative and most gracious. Exceptions to this rule are so rare in my own experience as to be virtually nonexistent.

Peter O'Toole is the most exciting actor I ever worked with — and certainly one of the most durable. In *My Favorite Year*, he had several physically demanding scenes which required many retakes for the usual acting and non-acting (camera, sound, etc.) adjustments. In one of those scenes, Joe Bologna, Adolph Green (the seven-time Tony Award winner and multiple Academy Award-nominated author and lyricist of *Band Wagon*, *On the Town*, *Singin' in the Rain*, etc.), Mark Linn-Baker, Bill Macy, Anne DeSalvo and I are in a meeting in which Peter does a somersault onto the conference table and passes out. Peter not only insisted on doing the stunt himself to make the scene better, but did it many times until director Richard Benjamin had everything he needed. And of course that kind of talent, dedication and professionalism pays off. Peter received one of his seven (so far) Academy Award leading actor nominations for that performance. And he now has a well-deserved Lifetime Achievement Award from the Academy.

Even though professionalism alone doesn't win awards, it gets respect from peers on the job, and that respect does lead to more and better parts in increasingly important productions. It's one of the rules of the game.

■ *What is acting?*

Acting has been variously described as "believing," "truth-telling" and even "pretending." Gregory Peck (Best Actor Academy Award winner in *To Kill a Mockingbird*) called it "story telling." My friend Quinn Redeker, actor and Oscar-nominated screenwriter (*The Deer Hunter*), calls writing and acting "emotional architecture." The most popular definition of acting is the very descriptive "behaving truthfully in imaginary circumstances." I would have thought that to be a good, acceptable definition, except for an experience I had a few years ago.

For the past several years, when I am available, I have spent one morning a week in a Christian Science nursing facility in Los Angeles reading Bible lessons. The people attending the lessons are usually residents or patients, but sometimes staff members and family members also listen in. On one particular occasion, when I had finished reading, a nicely dressed, mature gentleman came up to me and said, "I think I'm going to need some assistance." I told him that the nurses were coming right away. He laughed and said, "No, no, not that kind of assistance. I drove here from Altadena (a suburb of Los

Angeles), and I'm afraid I've forgotten how to get back on the freeway." I said that I couldn't help, but I would get him some directions. I told one of the nurses that there was someone needing assistance. The nurse said, "That's why I'm here." I laughed (as the other fellow had laughed) and said, "No, he doesn't need that kind of assistance. He drove here from Altadena, and he just needs some directions to get back to the freeway." The nurse looked at me and smiled. "He didn't drive here. He just thinks he drove here. He's a resident here — room 107. I'll take him back to his room." That gentleman was, indeed, behaving truthfully in imaginary circumstances. But delusional behavior is not acting, and a person who believes that an imaginary event is occurring in real life is not an actor.

Acting is many things, but for one concise description of *good* acting, this is my definition:
Acting is disciplined truthful behavior in contrived situations.

Discipline is a vital aspect of acting because the acting moment must be repeatable. On stage, the entire performance will be repeated every night. In film and television, each moment of each scene may be repeated dozens of times, with no connection to the moments that precede or follow it — and it has to be truthful *every* time.

■ *Is acting a craft or an art?*

The craft of acting is what the actor studies and practices. The art of acting is what a small minority of actors ever produces and, even then, *only if they are very, very good at their craft.* Artful acting will never result from a superficial, glib or narrowly focused approach to the actor's work.

An actor can become an efficient craftsman and have a successful career by marketing only his most commercial qualities, and it isn't a bad thing for an actor to do that if he has something that is readily marketable. It is also possible to become a better, more flexible and more truthful actor after achieving success with a limited range of skills. Many actors have managed to do that, and that growth may actually be necessary for the career to have longevity. But efficient craftsmanship and marketability do not, in and of themselves, have anything to do with art.

Unfortunately, most actors don't have immediately obvious marketable qualities (such as extreme good looks, natural comic gifts or easily recognizable and usable regional or ethnic looks, speech and behavior), so their roads to success depend on a more truthful course of study. The fervent quest for truth is a likely path to artistic achievement. I believe that *every* actor has the capacity to achieve some level of artistry if he sets that goal for himself and makes the necessary commitment to the truthfulness of his work.

■ *Should acting be like real life?*

No. Acting has to be *better* than real life. A person in real life has no obligation to communicate anything to anybody. He is not required to speak clearly, gesture meaningfully, nor to relate fully and appropriately to either his surroundings or to other people — and he has no need to be particularly interesting. Furthermore, he is not expected to repeat moments of his life, especially not at the discretion of some other person.

A character in a play or on film, however, must communicate *everything* (including, if necessary, his inability to communicate) with total clarity. Everything the character does has some purpose. His relationships to other characters and to his environment must be clear. And everything he does will have to be repeated, perhaps dozens or even hundreds of times.

■ *What is "Amplified Realism"?*

Amplify: (1) to expand by clarifying detail. (2) to make larger or more powerful. —*Webster's New Collegiate Dictionary*

"Amplified Realism" is the expression I use to describe the *result* of truthful acting. It is the goal of truthful acting. Amplified Realism is what the audience sees when the actor has done his work properly. What the audience must never see is the *process* of study, discovery, experimentation and rehearsal that result in truthful character behavior.

■ *Is film (camera) acting different from stage acting?*

There is neither film acting nor stage acting. There is only acting. All the differences are specific to individual acting situations. Every theatre is different from every other theatre, and every camera shot is different from every other camera shot.

When you see a theatre performance that has been filmed, and the performances are transparently phony, don't delude yourself into thinking that those performances probably looked truthful on the stage. They did not. Many years ago, my experience in a production of *South Pacific*, at Jones Beach in New York, provided a great example of what *not* to do just to fill a bigger space. Because the Jones Beach Theatre had 8,200 seats, I got the bright idea about halfway through the run that I needed to make my performance bigger. The audience members sitting some distance from the stage (probably 7,000 of them) couldn't see enough for my "improved" performance to make any difference. They were the lucky ones. Those who could see what I was doing must have been mystified by what they saw. Fortunately, I came to my senses long before the end of the run.

It is not helpful for the actor to think that a mechanical process of making it bigger or smaller or making it louder or softer will somehow magically be transformed into a non-mechanical, truthful moment. The character must be served, and the only way to achieve that end is by allowing the character to deal with the situation.

Academy Award winner Sir John Gielgud (*Arthur*), one of the great actors of the twentieth century (and whom I had the good fortune to see on stage five times), gave one of the best film performances I ever saw, *in a Broadway play*. The play was *Ivanov*, also starring two-time Academy Award-winning actress Vivien Leigh (*Gone with the Wind* and *A Streetcar Named Desire*). From my seat in the second row, I marveled at how intimate and real his performance was, and I wondered how he could possibly be heard in the back of that large theatre. What nonsense. John Gielgud could be heard in the back of every theatre he ever played in. Everything he did and said in that play was crystal clear to everyone in the theatre, *because the character needed to be seen and heard*. And he didn't have to sacrifice truthfulness for it.

There are, of course, necessary differences between film and stage acting that are based on preparation and rehearsal. But those differences are only reflected in the *approach* to the work. Film acting makes three demands on the actor that stage acting doesn't. First, the lines need to be memorized before the first rehearsal. Second, the actor's process of character discovery has to be accelerated considerably so that the character that emerges for the first day of shooting is the same character throughout the film. Finally, the character must be able to live and relive the briefest (and, sometimes, the most emotional) moments of his life, disconnected by days or weeks from preceding moments and even out of sequence, with truthful clarity. Conversely, film doesn't require the actor to play the entire script in two hours. A good actor should adapt relatively easily to the requirements of stage or film whenever he undertakes the work, *and homework is the key*.

■ *What is slick acting?*

Slick acting, sometimes called stock acting or formula acting, creates the character based on the actor's preconceived decision about the *type* of character (greedy industrialist, gangster, drunkard, farmer, etc.) he is. All the character's behaviors, including vocal inflections, mannerisms and gestures, are formed early and are based on the actor's ability and experience at playing that type of character. The slick characterization is frequently formed before the lines are memorized — and finalized (so that no part of it ever changes) before the first rehearsal. Slick acting doesn't even require the actor to read the entire script (traditionally, actors in stock weren't given the whole script, but instead received sides, their own character's lines preceded by the last few words of the cue line from another character).

On the positive side, slick actors (who are usually good craftsmen) are very employable because directors can depend on them to deliver solid, professional performances.

On the negative side, their work is never unique or insightful because it has no relationship to the specific, individual humanity of the character they are playing, but only to the general character type. Nor does slick acting allow for the possibility of surprises in character growth and development. Unfortunately, the glib nature of the work frequently leaves giant gaps in logic when important character or plot facts are overlooked or disregarded by the actor's rush to wrap up his performance.

A perfect example of just such a gaffe occurs in the motion picture *Laura*, when the detective, played by Dana Andrews, finds the shotgun murder weapon, removes the empty shell, and returns the gun to its hiding place inside a grandfather clock. When the murderer, played by the usually excellent Clifton Webb, retrieves the weapon and opens it, he doesn't react to the missing shell. If he had read the entire script, he would have known that his character had left the spent shell inside the shotgun, and he would have wondered where it went. But it is quite possible that Clifton Webb decided that he knew how to play the character because he had played that *type* of character so many times before, making the specifics of that particular character's life unnecessary for him to deal with. Unfortunately, this time he was wrong, creating a glaring leap of logic which might have caused some members of the audience to wonder if the *director* had read the script. Unfortunately (but often correctly), when these leaps of logic occur, most of the audience will wonder about the actor.

Even though there are many creative eyes on the work, including the director's, the script supervisor's (called "continuity" in Great Britain), the cinematographer's, the editor's and others, the person ultimately responsible for all aspects of the actor's performance is the actor. It is his face (and his career and his reputation) on the screen.

In the rare instances in which a script has been changed after the actor's related scenes have already been filmed, obviously the actor can't alter his completed work to conform to the script changes (and he might not even know that the changes were made). Ideally, an actor needs unflagging commitment and patience to do the sometimes tedious homework necessary to reach for completeness of character, rather than attempting to achieve certainty without availing himself of the crucial information that is readily available to him.

■ *What is autobiographical acting?*

Autobiographical acting (or egocentric acting) is a term used to describe acting that has nothing to do with the script or the character, but rather expresses the actor's own thoughts and feelings. Some training methods actually encourage the actor to interpret the material in terms of his own style of existence, in effect rewriting it to suit himself without regard for the writer's intentions or the character's life.

Autobiographical actors are easy to recognize in rehearsals by certain expressions they use to identify their acting approach. Expressions like "*I* would never say that" and "*I* would never do that" are dead giveaways. In performance, autobiographical acting is more difficult to spot unless the observer is familiar with either the material (which will have been distorted) or the actor's body of work (which will have a recurring sameness to it).

Because of the very truthfulness (but not necessarily character appropriateness) of autobiographical acting (at its best), some excellent directors have occasionally made use of the personal nature of this approach (especially when non-professional actors have been chosen for their strong personal emotional attachment to the material). Unfortunately, nonprofessionals cannot be reliably counted on to deliver performances that are up to professional standards.

Director Paul Greengrass's extensive use of autobiographical acting in his compelling film *United 93* produced mixed results. The nonprofessional actors who portrayed themselves were all quite effective when reacting to the urgency of the events, but most were unbelievable when called upon to reflect and converse with each other (as actors are required to do all the time), apparently improvisationally, about those events. Most notable in these lapses were their almost casual, untruthfully acted interjections about the rarity of airline hijackings (oddly inappropriate, as if one would take the time to ponder about the frequency of neighborhood fires after being informed that his neighbor's house was ablaze).

As examples of autobiographical acting used appropriately to better overall effect, I cite the remarkable first-time performances elicited from Lamberto Maggiorani in director Vittorio De Sica's *The Bicycle Thief*, Harold Russell (Academy Award winner) in director William Wyler's *The Best Years of our Lives* and Haing S. Ngor (Academy Award winner) in director Roland Joffe's *The Killing Fields*.

■ *What are the differences between audition, rehearsal and performance acting?*

Each audition, rehearsal and performance should incorporate and demonstrate the actor's best, most complete understanding of the character and his situation up to that point in the development of the role.

In rehearsal, the actor is assured of an opportunity to do the scene again. Each rehearsal should be used to integrate and reinforce changes that result from homework and from the previous rehearsal.

Most of the growth in the development of a role comes from homework, and each new aspect of the character needs to be revealed in the rehearsal that follows.

Auditions and performances offer no guarantees of second chances. An auditioning actor can't count on a directed replay or a callback. Any given performance of a play might be its last (and it is the last as far as most of the audience members are concerned). In film and television, each take might be the actor's last on-camera performance of that moment.

Professionalism demands complete work at the highest level every time out, in every audition, rehearsal or performance. In every case, the actor has to play the part with the certitude and totality of a moment in life that is experienced once, never to be repeated.

■ Is classical acting different from acting in more contemporary works?

It shouldn't be. Truthfulness is paramount. Subjective Situation Perception and Cornerstones of Truth, which appear elsewhere in this text, will lead the actor to that truthfulness in every character, in every script.

Even though the unfamiliarity of the language may present some difficulties, the honesty of the character's speech must be complete. The character's words must always be real human speech. William Shakespeare, himself, demanded it. As Hamlet instructs his players, "*Speak* the speech...." Take Shakespeare's word for it.

■ What is "at-oneness"?

When I speak of "at-oneness," I mean the *subjective* experience of acting. As an actor, you are not an observer commenting on the character's life; you are *in* the character's life. You *experience* the character's life. You are *at one* with the character.

For a perfect demonstration of at-oneness, I refer actors to the Academy Award-winning performance of Charlize Theron in *Monster*, all the more remarkable because the actress and the character are so obviously physically different (and seemingly different in many other respects as well). It is one of the better, completely realized, truthful performances on film. Obviously, the impact of the work is further enhanced when the actor appears to disappear completely into the character. Other examples (among many others) that come to mind are Daniel Day-Lewis (Academy Award winner) in *My Left Foot*, Hilary Swank in *Boys Don't Cry* (her first Academy Award – her second was for *Million Dollar Baby*), Geoffrey Rush (Academy Award winner) in *Shine*, Forest Whitaker in *The Last King of Scotland*, and the brilliant work of Sir Alec Guinness (Academy Award winner for *Bridge on the River Kwai*) in *Tunes of Glory*, which included a fine performance by Sir John Mills (an Academy Award winner in *Ryan's Daughter*).

I also recommend some excellent portrayals (among many, many others) of despicable, evil and violent individuals by Robert Mitchum in *Cape Fear*, Lee J. Cobb in *On the Waterfront* and Academy Award winners Ernest Borgnine (*Marty*) in *From Here to Eternity*, Morgan Freeman (*Million Dollar Baby*) in *Street Smart* and Sir Ben Kingsley (*Gandhi*) in *Sexy Beast*, for their at-oneness with their malevolent creations.

■ How important is imagination in acting?

Imagining is critical to the process of acting, as well as to the result as it is experienced by the audience. The actor must be able to imagine himself as another person, living that person's life, completely and unself-consciously, with all the specific thoughts, feelings and behavior of that person. It is only the actor's imagination that makes possible his total immersion into the character.

Are there special techniques for playing comedy?

These are six principles that I believe are essential to comedy:

1. Find the humor. An actor in comedy has to see humor in many situations, including some that seem inherently unfunny because that is where the funniest stuff often happens. The best comedy writers (Neil Simon and Woody Allen, for instance) have turned gloomy events into great comedies.

2. Be serious. The character is seriously involved in the moment. He doesn't know it's funny (unless he is joking).

3. Be bold. Fill the moment. In comedy, the audience must see Amplified Realism.

4. Be clear and clean. Words and actions in comedy must be crystal clear. Nowhere else in acting is respect for the writer's words more critical. And the audience must see and hear each moment. *In order for this to work, the audience must be aware of nothing else.* Distracting an audience during a comedy moment kills the moment.

5. Don't insult the audience. See Principle 6.

6. Allow the audience to laugh. Avoid reverential treatment of the material (Anton Chekhov's plays have suffered from this, perhaps more than the work of any other writer). If it's funny, let it be funny. Allowing the audience to laugh is not the same as asking for the laugh (they won't) or telling them that you expect them to laugh (they won't). If it's funny, they'll laugh.

III. DECISIONS ON TRAINING

THE FIRST QUESTION every actor should ask himself before making any move toward the pursuit of a professional career is, "How badly do I want this?" The reply should be, "I am willing to do whatever it takes to get it (without jeopardizing my health, safety or self respect)." No other answer is likely to produce a satisfactory outcome, no matter how great the talent. Having chosen acting as a career, training is the first and maybe the most important single step toward that goal.

A beginning actor who aspires to the highest levels of the business needs to understand what that means in the most practical terms. The fact is that actors who get to the career level where they actually contend for the important roles (every job that pays big money or opens the door to the jobs that do) in New York and Los Angeles may find himself in competition with the best actor in the world (at his level of experience) for that role. Actors should approach the subject of training with that fact in mind.

■ *What are the most important attributes for someone who wants an acting career?*

The words that most come to mind when I think of the qualities most necessary to train for, to begin, and to sustain an acting career are desire, courage, commitment, enthusiasm and persistence. An actor who has those five attributes can overcome all obstacles. If those qualities are lacking, to achieve even a modest degree of success would require more than a great deal of luck (a concept that enjoys a wide acceptance, even though it has never been satisfactorily explained to me).

■ *Why is training necessary?*

Every good professional actor you ever heard of studied acting. Despite anecdotes to the contrary, they all studied somewhere, in schools, in classes, with private teachers, or by intensive immersion into the acting (or other performing) profession. *There are so few exceptions to this axiom that beginning actors would do well to regard the exceptions as nonexistent.* No matter where they studied, or with whom, they all learned the craft. An actor who aspires to succeed must regard the learning of his craft as the foundation of that future success, because the actors he will compete with on a daily basis have all been trained. Obviously, if an actor has not been blessed with an overabundance of talent, good looks and good fortune, then the quality of the training is even more important. And dedication is critical.

■ *What do my goals have to do with my training choices?*

Having made the decision to act, every actor needs to decide what his goals are. Even though these goals will likely change many times over the course of one's career, the goals have to be clear. The character Bloody Mary in *South Pacific* explained it best when she sang, "You got to have a dream. If you don't have a dream, how you gonna have a dream come true?" An unfocused actor, even if he is fortunate, will likely find himself doing a little bit of everything, but not much of anything. The object is to do much.

There are two categories of acting goals, and they only have to do with jobs. The first category, the short term goal, is to get an acting job. The second category, the long term goal, is to have an acting career. The most accessible jobs are always those for which the actor's talents are best suited, so it is in the actor's best interest to set his initial sights in that direction. Examples of acting goals include Broadway, film and television, musical theatre, repertory and soap operas.

■ *Where should I go to study?*

Most of the best teachers and coaches are in Los Angeles and New York because that is where the highest level of the industry is. Therefore, that is where the demand for good teachers and coaches is the greatest. Furthermore, the best actors are in Los Angeles and New York, and some of them teach. The more removed a teacher is from the acting business and the more removed his experience is from the professional acting experience, the greater the possibility that his teaching may be less practical than what the profession requires. *This is not a rule.* There are, and always will be, exceptions to this generalization, many talented and inspirational teachers in other cities whose students enter the profession extremely well prepared and then proceed to have important careers. Some teachers and teaching programs outside of the two great acting centers are so highly regarded for their work that their reputations reach far beyond their own communities. I urge actors to seek out and avail themselves of those training opportunities when New York and Los Angeles are not workable options. It is also important that actors get as much acting experience as they can wherever they can (high school, college, community theatre, etc.) before undertaking the serious life change that a commitment to the profession usually demands.

The quality and quantity of teacher choices available in Los Angeles and New York are pretty much the same. However, the actor's goals should have considerable influence on his choice of a city in which to study *and work*. Presumably, the actor will choose to study where most of his prospective employment is.

An actor who intends to focus on film and television, including soap operas, should study in Los Angeles, not because film acting is different from stage acting, but because teachers and coaches will likely have valuable industry experiences that they can impart to the actors who study with them, and most film and television work (by a long shot), including most of the soap operas, is in Los Angeles.

Actors whose skills and ambitions lead them toward live theatre should study in New York, not only because New York is the most important theatre center in the United States, but also because it's where most of the good singing and dancing instruction is.

A word of caution: Just as most of the good acting teachers are in New York and Los Angeles, so are many of the bad ones. Choose carefully.

■ *How do I find a good school or teacher?*

The most important criteria for judging the quality of an acting school or teacher are ideas, communication and chemistry. The concepts need to be new to the actor so that the actor is not wasting his time, and they must be truthful so that they are applicable to every acting experience. The ideas must be conveyed so clearly to the actor that he understands them *immediately.* And the teacher's personality has to be so nurturing and trust-inspiring that the actor is immediately able to *experience and demonstrate* the principle in the scene or monologue he is working on. *The actor must demand immediate demonstrable results from the teacher and from himself. Immediacy in this context means that the actor must understand, assimilate and begin to demonstrate obvious, tangible results within the first thirty minutes of practical work with the teacher's acting concepts.*

It is also crucial that the actor is given sufficient time in every class to reinforce the newly absorbed enlightenment. Acting is not like geometry. It can't be learned by listening to a lecture or by watching someone else trying to work it out. It must be experienced, rehearsed and re-rehearsed under the patient scrutiny of the teacher. The actor must know how the process feels, and when he has accomplished that, he must know that he knows it.

The best, most obvious qualification for an acting teacher is professional acting experience. The second best qualification is professional directing experience. Obviously, there are good teachers without either of those qualifications. *Nevertheless, it is important that the teacher has the ability to effectively and successfully demonstrate what he teaches.*

Don't choose an acting teacher just because you think he might hire you someday. Agent, manager and casting director showcases and workshops are valuable for purposes of gaining exposure for representation and employment. Experienced casting directors, in particular, can offer invaluable insight into actors' presentation techniques that succeed (and those that don't). Agents, managers and casting directors, *if they have the appropriate acting or directing experience*, would be good potential acting teachers or coaches because of their useful knowledge about the business aspects of the business. However, agenting, managing or casting experience, in and of themselves, wouldn't be qualifications to teach acting, any more than an actor's extensive exposure to agents, managers and casting directors would qualify that actor to teach agenting, managing or casting.

To my knowledge, there is no one best way to find a good teacher or school. Here are some of the good ways:

1. Recommendations from actors who have taken a class or course. Always consider the source of the recommendation.

2. Recommendations from people you should respect who have heard of the school or teacher.

3. Brochures and other published materials and advertisements from the school, including the names of well-known alumni.

4. Internet research (including blogs generated by actors and other industry professionals).

5. Bookstores that service the theatrical community.

You must not commit yourself or your money to a long-term training situation unless you are sure that it is right for you. You must be allowed to observe (audit) the class, or, in the case of an acting school, audit a portion of every class. You need to know that your most important personal criteria are fulfilled, so that the material covered and the teacher's approach will be useful to you in developing your craft in pursuit of the kinds of jobs that you want. If auditing is not offered, then a money-back guarantee should be.

Recommendations, long waiting lists and impressive alumni rosters are not always reliable guides to good training. Trust your own personal responses to what you see and hear in the school or class.

■ Can an actor be permanently harmed by destructive teachers and teaching methods?

Probably not, but it is vitally important for the acting student to escape from those situations before *any* damage is done. Unfortunately, even the best research doesn't necessarily produce a predictable outcome, so it behooves the actor to avoid lingering in training situations after unfavorable aspects begin to reveal themselves. The more exposure one has to incapable or even vicious teachers, the longer it might take to overcome the negative effects. But no damage needs to be permanent.

When I began my actor training in New York, I attended a prestigious conservatory for two years. Because I was one of the one-third of the junior year class who had been invited back for the final year, I believed that my work had been satisfactory. Unfortunately, I didn't know then that my own feelings of confusion and frustration were danger signs that the training I had been receiving was causing damage to my creative process, and I, like so many other beginning actors, allowed myself to be guided by what I *thought* my teachers saw in me. What a mistake.

Shortly after the beginning of my second year, I heard that one of the directors had started to admonish his students against a certain kind of work (I never learned what that kind of work was), referring to it as the "Basil Hoffman School of Acting." I was shocked and deeply hurt. I believe that pain and the pain I felt from yet another negative school-related experience stayed with me for several years after I left that school and entered the profession.

The second incident occurred after I graduated and managed to get myself an interview with the casting director for the important Stratford, Connecticut, Shakespeare Festival. The casting director looked at my resume and noted the name of the school I had just left. She said, "Why weren't you on the list of graduating students that the school sent me?" Of course, I had no answer. Obviously the associate director of the school, who had prepared the list, thought that I would be unfit for any role in that company. Consequently, the Stratford casting director concluded that there was no need to audition me, and the interview was over.

Regardless of the negative impact that those experiences had on me, many years later I continue to have a successful career. My advice to beginning actors is to be more vigilant and respectful of your own feelings than I was. But even if you suffer some emotional setback, know that it is only temporary. After all, the Basil Hoffman School of Acting has thrived for a long time, and it has proven successful not only for me, but for many others as well.

■ *Should I accept acting jobs before I finish my training?*

The ultimate purpose of study is to acquire the necessary skills to get acting jobs, *and to get those jobs*. Generally speaking, the better the jobs, the better the skills needed to get those jobs. But better acting skills don't guarantee better jobs. When offered acting work during a course of study, the actor needs to weigh the importance of the job (the prestige of the project), the importance of the role, the money and whether the job will even interfere with the actor's course of study, against the value and the urgency of the training. I offer examples of correct work decisions by two actors I have known and worked with.

The great Jason Robards (Academy Award winner in *All the President's Men* and *Julia*) abandoned the second year of a two-year course at the American Academy of Dramatic Arts, in favor of acting jobs off and on Broadway that started a distinguished 60-year career. Perry King, while a student at Juilliard, was offered a part in a film. He asked the founder and head of the acting program, John Houseman (Supporting Actor Academy Award winner in *The Paper Chase*), whether or not he should leave school and accept the job. Houseman's response was, "When you can work, work. When you can't work, study." Perry took that advice, and that job, which was the title role in *The Possession of Joel Delaney*, also starring Shirley MacLaine (Academy Award winner in *Terms of Endearment*), launched an important career.

■ *What is the difference between teaching and coaching, and are teachers and coaches the same people?*

Teaching is the process designed to improve the actor's skills in a way that they may be applied to every future acting (or singing or dancing, etc.) situation. A good acting teacher doesn't really teach acting, but, rather, makes the actor aware of the possibilities of obedience to truthfulness. Many professional actors continue the study of their craft throughout their careers (singers, dancers and musicians never stop training), although, unfortunately, there are many who do not.

Coaching, as the term is generally used, means preparation for a specific role (for audition, rehearsal or performance purposes). In my opinion, good coaching imparts lasting principles, in much the same way that good teaching does, in ways the actor can use every time he approaches a new part.

Teachers and coaches are not necessarily the same people. Most acting coaches are also teachers. Most teachers, however, aren't coaches. A good teacher will promote tangible *progress* in the actor's growth in every session. However, the teacher's goal isn't the performance, but rather the process. Coaches are held to a much higher standard because they are required to produce tangible results very quickly.

President of the United States Ronald Reagan once described the studio's priorities when he was an actor under contract to Warner Brothers. "They didn't want it good. They wanted it Thursday." For the actor (and the acting coach), the requirements are somewhat different. Having it Thursday isn't enough. *It also better be good.*

Actors need to demand constant, demonstrable progress from themselves in their study. A teacher (or coach) who doesn't facilitate demonstrable results should be terminated (fired, not murdered). Actors frequently prolong their exposure to inadequate training. Time is precious and fleeting. Don't squander it in frustration and confusion. There are good teachers and coaches, and there are right ones for you.

■ *Should I lose my accent?*

The most obvious answer to this question is yes, except that there are many examples of successful careers of actors who have *chosen* to retain their native foreign accents (and regional American dialects) while working in American films. I have a few thoughts to offer actors who have this particular decision to face.

First, the positives of retaining an accent. Many casting directors and directors are attracted by native accents and dialects because those particular characteristics of speech are also truthful elements of character. If character is the first and by far the most important element in any performance (and it is), then any truthful ingredient in that characterization would be expected to have a positive effect. Furthermore, a truthful accent is easier than truthful acting for some directors and casting directors to recognize, so that an accent is often a winning attention-getter.

Many star actors have retained their native accents because their early successes seemed to celebrate those accents, even when the actors' natural accents are inappropriate (and unexplained) for the characters the actors are playing. I would include in this star category the deceptively versatile Cary Grant (possibly the most watchable movie star of all time) and, except in very rare instances, Academy Award winners Sissy Spacek (*Coal Miner's Daughter*), Joe Pesci (*Goodfellas*), Tommy Lee Jones (*The Fugitive*) and Robert DeNiro (*The Godfather: Part II* and *Raging Bull*). It is interesting to observe that a number of previous Academy Award nominees later won the awards for roles in which they uniquely abandoned their native accents, including Al Pacino in *Scent of a Woman*, Rod Steiger in *In the Heat of the Night*, Michael Caine in *The Cider House Rules* (his second Academy Award, the first being for *Hannah and Her Sisters*) and Holly Hunter in *The Piano* (in which she was completely silent).

Unfortunately, the legions of actors whose careers were needlessly limited by retaining their regionalisms will have to remain nameless. Conversely, it is impossible to know how many careers have been considerably helped by actors' ability to lose (at least temporarily) the regionalisms or foreign accents they were brought up with.

One notable foreign-born actor (among many others) whose success has been enhanced by his facility with standard American speech is Rutger Hauer, who received acclaim in the Dutch language film *Soldier of Orange* and has since enjoyed a long, successful American and international career. Academy Award-winning director Woody Allen (*Annie Hall*) has repeatedly made use of foreign-born actors with skilled American dialects, including Academy Award nominees Tim Roth (British), Helena Bonham Carter (British) and Judy Davis (Australian), who has worked with Allen four times. Russell Crowe (New Zealand-Australia), who became a star as an American policeman in *L.A. Confidential* before winning an Academy Award in *Gladiator*, has also benefited greatly from his ability to sound American.

The standard American dialect that is adaptable to the vast majority of roles has improved the castability of a countless number of American actors, as well, who might not have been fortunate enough to find just the roles that would have given them fame as regional characters.

A good rule of thumb to follow when making the decision to retain or lose an accent would be an honest self-assessment of the number of roles that would be appropriate for you, given your looks and physicality, with or without the accent. Bear in mind that you can always call upon it when you need it, but it might not be so easy to get people to visualize you without it if they have come to believe that the accent is a permanent part of you.

IV. APPROACHES TO ▪▪
TRAINING

THE QUALITY OF WORK the actor produces *depends* on his approach to the study of his craft. That approach includes his choice of teachers and coaches, his diligence at homework, and his fearlessness and painstaking preparation in class work.

The selection of a teacher or school, given the care the actor should have exercised in that selection, will have a profound influence on the kind of an actor he becomes and the amount of time it takes him to become that kind of actor. Of course, an inappropriate teacher choice can be terminated at any time, sooner rather than later, and the selection process revisited. An actor would be well advised to have a very low tolerance to class time endured without *significant* progress (*and only the actor, not his teacher and his peers, can be the judge of that progress*). Confusion and frustration are reliable symptoms of unsatisfactory teaching.

Homework, daily and purposeful, is required even when the actor isn't involved in a formal course of study. Reading aloud (subjectively only), memorizing monologues, studying dialects, watching acting performances with a specifically critical eye, and observing human speech and behavior are good subjects for private study. However, the actor is cautioned against rehearsing and reinforcing untruthful work. To insure against that, the actor needs to have acquired a working knowledge of what is truthful, and what is not. Contrary to a widely held belief, practice does not always make perfect. Only correct practice makes perfect (and, even then, only theoretically).

For the actor who is taking a class, privately or with other actors, doing enough homework to fulfill the assignment is only the acceptable minimum. Doing even more than that is better. And homework needs to be done on the actor's own time, not during class time. Being well prepared in class accomplishes four things. First, preparedness gives the actor courage to perform. Second, it is a demonstration of respect for the teacher (and the other actors, if there are other actors). Third, it informs the teacher of the actor's progress. And, finally, it moves the actor forward in the improvement of his craft.

Neglecting the craft is a mistake at any stage of a career. At the beginning of a career it can be ruinous.

■ *What is the fallacy of scene study?*

The fallacy of scene study (as the term is generally used) is the belief that rehearsing two (or more) actors in a scene is the most efficient format for training actors. Unfortunately, that form of scene study neglects character development and gives no attention to the hearing of inner cues. Furthermore, it places undue emphasis on rehearsing one particular scene with one particular acting partner (as if repetitive rehearsal would magically reveal character), a situation which has limited applicability to other scenes with other actors, and which never replaces private character study in the real world of acting, where the actor might never have even met his scene partner(s) before he arrives on the set to shoot the scene.

Professional actors do not develop their characterizations and the feelings and behavior of their characters based on the work of other actors. They do that work at home, a process that is impossible for actors who have not yet sufficiently learned their craft.

■ *What is the value of improvisation?*

When the actor is working on a role, improvisation, the physical (not written) creation of an unscripted scene, can be a useful homework and rehearsal technique. However, the character in the improvisation must be the same character as the one in the script. Otherwise, the improvisation exercise is counterproductive to the actor's character work.

Improvisational work independent of any particular script can be used by an actor to experience a range of feelings by doing different tasks with a variety of specific motivations. If the process stretches the actor's ability to behave spontaneously (unpreparedly) in contrived (prepared) situations, it is valuable.

■ *What is "monologue power"?*

"Monologue power" is what I believe to be inherent in speech spoken to a character or characters who, for whatever reason, remain silent. It is a powerful form for teaching and learning acting because it releases the actor from dependence on the personality, performance or whims of any other actor (and from any comfort that might be derived from working with that actor) and from being victimized by unforeseen circumstances of auditions, rehearsals and performances. It forces the actor to be so knowledgeable about his character and so immersed in the character's life that the character becomes responsible for his own behavior, no matter what happens.

For teaching purposes, I have a number of criteria that I impose on an actor's selection of an appropriate monologue. Here are those criteria and the reasons why they are important to me:

1. The monologue must be in contemporary English.
    This doesn't rule out good English translations of the plays of Anton Chekhov, Henrik Ibsen, Federico Garcia Lorca, August

Strindberg, Jean-Paul Sartre, Michel de Ghelderode, Eugene Ionesco, and many, many other non-English language writers, as long as the material requires no particular understanding of period and place. I demand contemporary English and contemporary milieu because I don't want the actor to be saddled with intricacies of unfamiliar custom and syntax. Obviously, at some point in his work, the actor will need to confront those issues. But that should happen only for the *purpose* of dealing with those issues. For the actor who wants to strengthen his craft, truthful feelings and behavior should be his only concerns.

2. The monologue must be from a published or produced work (play, screenplay, teleplay, novel, short story).

I include this requirement because I want the actor to become familiar with the process of reading and investigating the entire work to discover vital character information not contained in the monologue (and maybe not even in any of the scenes in which the character appears). This process is essential to the actor's work in the profession, so it should become an integral part of his training.

3. The monologue must be spoken to another person (*one person*) who is alive, and present and able to respond, even though, in this particular scene, the other person is silent.

These three requirements are necessary for my purposes because in life there is no predictability of the behavior of other people. Likewise, the character speaking a monologue doesn't know if or when the other character or characters will speak, or how they will behave. It only turns out to be a monologue because the character speaks uninterruptedly. But he has no way of knowing before he finishes speaking that that will be the case. The actor cannot allow the character to know more than logic would allow the character to know.

4. The subject and content of the monologue must be important in the life of the character.

   The more problematic and personal the circumstance is for the character, the better I like it. I want actors to be willing and able to find the emotional stuff in every role they play, so it is important that they get used to approaching the work from that aspect. *Every* character has an emotional life. It is the actor's responsibility to discover what those feelings are and how the character demonstrates them through words and actions.

5. The monologue must be of sufficient length (at least one and one-half to two minutes) to give the character an opportunity to demonstrate some range of his thoughts and feelings.

6. Except for cold reading purposes, the monologue must be memorized.

V. CHARACTER STUDY ▪

CHARACTER STUDY is the process of investigation and discovery that reveals the person inside the character the writer created, and brings him to life. In that process, the actor becomes the *author* of the character's living feelings and behavior (and words), just as the writer is the reporter of that information.

Every character in literature is a complete person. But in literature, the character engages the audience only insofar as the writer is able to stimulate the reader's imagination. The actor's work turns that literary concept into a visible and audible person, and the more multifaceted and real that person is, the more compelling he is to watch. *All aspects of the character's behavior are the actor's responsibility.*

Whether or not character descriptions are contained explicitly or implicitly in the written material, the actor needs to find as much truthful personal information about the character as he can, and incorporate it into the work. Character, revealed and developed in the homework process, is the part of the actor's work that brings real life to the writer's creation. Without fullness of character, acting is only a report of the scripted material (as if the audience couldn't buy the script and read it for themselves for much less money and inconvenience). Character is the real magic of acting.

A good actor strives for completion of character not only for the fulfillment of his own character but to engage the other characters within his sphere, which elevates the work of every actor he works with. Even though each actor does his own character work, the depth of character work done by every other actor enriches his own.

■ *What is "Subjective Situation Perception," and why do I need to know about it?*

Subjective: (1) having to do with the perception or conception of a thing by the mind as opposed to its reality independent of the mind. (2) existing or originating within the observer's mind or sense organs and, hence, incapable of being checked externally or verified by other persons.
—*Webster's New Collegiate Dictionary*

"Subjective Situation Perception" is the term I use to describe human behavior and to outline (as succinctly as I can) the elements of life and environment that affect that behavior. *There is no other basis for truthful acting*.

Acting is subjective because human behavior is subjective. There is no outside, impartial, objective observer in human behavior. Human behavior is based upon and controlled by *subjective* perception, of the self and of the entire universe. If acting were objective, it would be called reporting. But it isn't called reporting. It's called acting. *In acting, the reality in every situation is only what the character perceives it to be*.

Even though I recognized a long time ago that truthful acting is based on the principle of subjectivity, I didn't give the subjective perception concept a name until I had to describe it to a non-actor. In October 1997, the U.S. Senate's Government Affairs Committee was investigating illegal contributions to the president's re-election campaign. I was contacted by a law firm in Washington, D.C., whose client had been subpoenaed to testify in the hearings. The lawyer had ascertained (correctly, I believe) that the client's hostile attitude toward the hearings and the investigation would not serve him well in responding to the committee's questions, and wanted me to prepare (coach) his client. (For legal and ethical reasons, I won't reveal the names of the attorneys or their client.) Subsequently, the lawyer visited me in Los Angeles with a non-disclosure agreement to protect the confidentiality of the information to which I was about to have access, and to outline a preparation strategy which I explained as the necessity of changing his client's *perception of the situation*.

I arrived in Washington several days before the client's scheduled appearance before the committee, although witnesses never know very far in advance what day they will actually testify. At my request, the lawyer arranged for me to attend one day's hearings so that I could get a firsthand look at the "set" (the hearing room) and the "players" (the senators on the committee and the witnesses and their attorneys). The entire structure of the hearings gives an advantage (they think) to the committee. The senators sit behind a long table on a platform, while the witnesses and their attorneys are seated behind tables on the floor several feet below them. And the committee knows the agenda and the specific questions, whereas the witnesses and their attorneys don't. Intimidating. Or so they want it to be.

My witness-to-be had accurately perceived that the committee's intention was to make political points at his (the witness's) expense, *to elicit information that only the witness had*, and to subject him to potential prosecution if they could. Being defensive, fearful, angry and victimized would have been a perfect characterization to fit into the scenario the committee had prepared, and which I will call *The D.A. Traps a Killer*. That role and that play, however, weren't suitable for my "actor."

So I devised a new play that we might entitle *The Patient Professor*. In the new script a brilliant professor finds himself assigned to instruct a special education class of low-I.Q. students *who know nothing*. The professor's task is to educate the students in only the very bare essentials by patiently answering only the questions the students ask. The attorneys and their client understood what I referred to as *subjective situation perception*, and they loved the new script.

The lawyers had prepared a long list of potential questions and rehearsed the client to provide very brief responses. I explained to the "professor" that his students required love and understanding, and those who asked the most questions, many of which had already been asked and answered, were actually the most mentally challenged students who required the most patience. The client fully accepted the premise and *enjoyed* the process because he was in control of it. His *perception* of the entire event had changed, *although in an objective sense nothing was different.*

In the hearing my witness was perfect. The senators on the committee, most of whom are used to feeling important, respected and elite, found themselves cast in quite different roles, which they hadn't expected but which they unwittingly played perfectly. The client's time in the hearing was much shorter than expected because his testimony and his attitude were counterproductive to the real aims of the committee.

I am gratified every time I see how quickly Subjective Situation Perception is understood and demonstrated, even by people who have no acting background but who grasp the concept because it relates directly to universal life experiences. It is for the very reason of truthfulness that actors need to know about the concept. Subjective Situation Perception defines the acting experience by these seven components:

1. WHO are you (the words "you" and "your" refer to the character, not to the actor) – your age, health, family and social background, geographic birth and upbringing, mental condition, education, vocation, avocations, military experience, financial circumstances, and most important, your essence? How does that affect your thoughts, your feelings, your words and your actions? Much of the information unearthed from the following six investigations will provide clues to the character's essence.

2. WHAT is the event (the happening or occasion) in which you find yourself? What happens in the course of that event? How

does that affect your thoughts, your feelings, your words and your actions?

3. WHERE is the event – what nation, what region, indoors or outdoors, wet weather or dry, comfortable temperature or uncomfortable, crowded or deserted, urban or rural, opulent or ramshackle, public or private, formal or informal, pleasant or unpleasant, familiar or unfamiliar, safe or dangerous? What are the non-human elements in that environment, including animate and inanimate nature, architecture and furnishings, mechanical objects and every other thing you are using, wearing, carrying or otherwise experiencing? How do those elements affect your thoughts, your feelings, your words and your actions?

4. WHEN does the event take place – the year, time of year, time of day, day or date or moment of particular significance? How does that affect your thoughts, your feelings, your words and your actions?

5. WHY are you there – your reasons and not the reasons of others? For example, you are at a party because your wife wanted you to go. But even if she asked you to go to the party, your reason for going is particular to your own thoughts and feelings about her request. You go because you love your wife and you like to see her happy, or because you love parties, or because you want to be with that particular group of people or because your wife is a bitch and you know that if you don't go you will have to endure interminable sulking and carping. What do you expect to happen, what do you want to happen and what actually occurs? How does that affect your thoughts, your feelings, your words and your actions?

6. WHERE were you (physically and mentally) before the scene starts? Where do you expect to be and where do you want to be

during the scene or after the scene ends? How does that affect your thoughts, your feelings, your words and your actions?

7. WHO are the other people (in the scene, in the rest of the script, referred to in the script, or implied in the script)? How do you speak to them and behave toward them? How do you expect them to behave toward you (and do they fulfill your expectations)? Are you aware of their behavior toward other people? How do you speak about them to other people? How do they behave toward you? How do they expect you to behave toward them (and do you fulfill their expectations)? How do they speak to you? What do they say about you to other people? How does that affect (or reflect) your thoughts, your feelings, your words and your actions?

The Subjective Situation Perception breakdown as I have outlined it provides a direct and complete guide to the discovery of character. Even though some of the elements may seem to have little or no effect on your character's thoughts, feelings or behavior, you can't know that until you have considered and investigated them.

■ *How does an actor begin work on a role?*

You always begin with a blank slate. The actor must begin by being open to hearing everything the character has to tell him, without superimposing preconceived decisions about the character based upon his own life (or acting) experiences.

Several years ago while we were working on *Comes a Horseman*, I asked Jason Robards, "What's the first thing you think when you read a new script?" His response was, "I don't know how to do this." So this great actor had to learn how to do it, every time he got a new role.

The first thing an actor must do with a new part is learn everything he can about that character. The best source for that information is the script. So the actor has to read the script, over and over again. Every reading of the script (at least the first three or four readings) will reveal some additional, important bit of information about the character's life and what effect it has on his feelings and behavior. I recommend that the actor use the Subjective Situation Perception concept as a guide to the kind of information he needs to look for, *and thoroughly research whatever is unfamiliar to him.*

■ *What are stage directions and narrative, and are they important to an actor's performance?*

The terms "stage directions" and "narrative" mean the same thing, and they serve the same purpose, but not in the same context. Stage directions is a theatrical term referring to the unspoken portion of a play's text, which describes the setting, the light and sound cues and the action of the play. Narrative is the film and television equivalent of stage directions, and it describes the time, place and action of the film and some of the thoughts and feelings of the characters.

An actor *needs* to read all the stage directions or narrative in a script as carefully as he reads the dialogue. Just as dialogue constitutes a character's verbal expression, so do stage directions and narrative contain references to the character's thoughts, feelings and physicality (when he moves and how he moves). Even though those references are seldom ironclad, they indicate some of the writer's thought processes in the creation of the character.

In film and television scripts particularly, writers frequently use narrative to describe behavior that illuminates important nuances of character, insights that might otherwise elude the actor. Narrative also includes the actions of other characters. Sometimes that information, even in scenes in which your character doesn't appear, might be critically important to your character's thoughts, feelings and behavior.

It is very important for an actor to make use of every bit of information available that helps him to develop his character. It is also important to ignore or discard information that isn't helpful, particularly physical descriptions of age, height, weight, sex, ethnicity and eye color that do not and cannot apply to you (unless there is a specific reason for you to incorporate those characteristics into the work). It is also a good idea to disregard descriptions of facial expressions, perspiration and heart rate. Let common sense and an open mind guide you to the information that is applicable and usable.

■ *What is a character's "essence," and why is it important for me to identify it?*

A character's "essence" is his fundamental core quality that is constantly projected. It is the force that ultimately determines the character's every thought, feeling, utterance and action. What *kind* of a person is he? How would you describe him after a brief initial meeting with him?

Frequently, the character's essence can be described by a single word, such as, for example, fearless, timid, dangerous, methodical, paranoid, frenzied or hostile. For all practical purposes, there is an infinite (virtually) number of words that may be used to define a character, but the more words an actor finds appropriate to his character's essence, the more muddled his conception of that character may become. A succinct description is likely to provide the greatest clarity. Finding the character's *demonstrable* essence is so vital to a successful performance that if the actor can't find a single, perfectly descriptive word, he should sit down with a dictionary or thesaurus until he finds it. If this process is at all frustrating, the actor needs to reread the script (with Subjective Situation Perception in mind) until the character reveals himself.

The character's behavior in every situation is controlled by his essence. It is important to identify the character's essence because every acting choice you make will depend on it. It will be the glue that holds your performance together in a cohesive, crystal clear characterization, regardless of the variety and severity of the character's conflicts and obstacles or the relative ease of his life. Your character's essence will determine, in large part, his posture, the way he walks and his manner of speech. His essence is his personal imprint.

Acting is subjective. Different actors approaching the same character may not be similarly informed about the essence of that character. Consequently, those actors will describe and demonstrate the character differently — and each actor's choice might be perfectly valid. There is a wide range of possible interpretations for every character, but every character choice has to be supported by the logic of the script.

All the clues to the essence of the character you are playing will be found somewhere in the material in which the character appears (but clues might be in *scenes* in which the character doesn't appear). Even though your character's essence must be something you can attain and sustain truthfully, none of the information about that character can be found in your own life, unless you happen to be the actual character.

Even when a script is written for you, it is not the same as having it written about you. Don't get confused. Keep your ego out of your character. He will reward you for it.

■ *Does the character's essence contain elements of the actor's essence?*

Ideally, the character's essence comes from the script (text and subtext), not from set or preconceived ideas (nor from a previously established acting style). However, in actuality, each actor brings his own life experiences and his own personality to every script, and that actor's ability (or inability) to sublimate his own personal characteristics will greatly affect the essence and the behavior of the character.

The roles an actor plays and the way he plays them frequently depend upon the range of the actor's abilities. For some actors, limited range doesn't retard the kinds of roles, the quality of the acting, the fame or the longevity of a career. Ability isn't the only factor. Sometimes an actor plays only certain kinds of parts and only plays them in a certain way because of his conscious choices. An actor who has a certain image because of his success in a particular vehicle may be reluctant to accept roles that are very different from the one that got him that notoriety.

Sometimes the industry makes those decisions for the actor, and producers and casting directors can't or don't want to see the actor in different parts, even though the actor wants to play them. In those cases, the actor either accepts the success he has or he takes extraordinary measures to get the opportunities he wants.

Even stars have sometimes had to plead to audition or screen test for roles believed to be inappropriate for them, and some have even altered their appearances to get those parts. When director Francis Ford Coppola wanted Academy Award winner Marlon Brando (*On the Waterfront*) to play Vito Corleone in *The Godfather*, Brando's perceived declining stardom and unpredictable behavior made him an unacceptable choice to the executives at Paramount. To convince the studio, Coppola went to Brando's house to film him in an improvised scene, for which Brando blackened his hair with shoe polish and puffed out his cheeks with cotton, making him unrecognizable. Brando's surprise performance in the test got him the job, and his performance in the picture won him another Academy Award. Francis Ford Coppola was nominated for the directing Oscar, and the film won the award for Best Picture.

■ *What is the difference between playing an attitude and playing a character, and are attitude and essence the same thing?*

Playing an attitude is an acting concept that restricts the character's responses in any given situation to whatever comes out of that one particular attitude. Fortunately, in life, people's attitudes do not determine who they are (and nobody goes through life with only one attitude at all times and in all situations). In fact, the reverse is true, in life and in acting. Even the most seemingly one-dimensional character has many personality facets. This is *always* true. It is the actor's challenge to find them.

Attitude and essence are not the same thing because attitude is only a momentary result of a character's reaction to some stimulus. That reaction depends, in large part, on the character's essence. The essence of a character is that dominant quality of personality from which all of his attitudes are formed.

■ *What constitutes the physicality of a character?*

Physicality refers to the ways that the character moves and positions his body. It also especially refers to facial expressions, since the face usually registers thoughts and feelings before the voice and body express them. The most commonplace physical activities, such as lying down, sitting up, sitting down, standing, gesturing, walking and running, reveal important aspects of character that plot and dialogue do not, and, furthermore, each of these physical activities provides an opportunity for the character to demonstrate some aspect of his uniqueness.

Essence of character may be revealed in physicality long before the character speaks or participates in any meaningful story line activity. In addition, the character's health and state of mind are reflected by his posture, his movements, and his facial expressions.

The physical character truthfully demonstrated engages the audience immediately and strengthens their involvement in events that follow.

Auditioning actors, especially, need to recognize the fact that the character's physicality is the first thing the audience sees. The physical demonstration of character, which begins before the character speaks, actually supports and reinforces everything else the actor does in the audition. Furthermore, that indelible first impression is an attention-getting moment that might determine the level of attention an audition receives and may ultimately decide whether or not the actor gets the job. For that reason alone, actors need to pay attention to this important element of character, not to mention the power that physicality imparts to every other aspect of the work.

■ *What does "living in the moment" mean and what is its importance?*

"Living in the moment" describes the process of mental and emotional responses that characterize the lives of human beings. If you are a real person and you are functioning at all, you are living in the moment, every day, all the time, *every moment*. The same is true for every character you play. He behaves in exactly the same way. The concept is vital to acting.

It is impossible to think or feel more than one thing in a single moment. Every individual moment has a complete life from beginning to end, and that momentary life is now, not one-tenth of a second ago and not one-tenth of a second from now. It is absolutely necessary that your character live each moment only in the present. It is impossible to live any part of a past moment because that moment is gone, and it is impossible to live any part of a future moment because it doesn't exist yet and your character can't possibly know about it. You can remember a past moment, *but the act of remembering is present* – and, while you can anticipate a future moment, *the act of anticipation is present.*

No matter how confused or conflicted a character may be, each moment contains only one thought, and the moment must be complete before the next moment occurs. A character involved in a love-hate relationship doesn't love and hate in the same moment; he loves in one moment and hates in the next. A character who can't make up his mind doesn't think two things in the same moment; he thinks one thing in one moment and something else in the next moment.

By allowing your character to fill each moment with a single, complete idea, you will give clarity to the character and the performance. Your character will be forced into specific thinking, and his resulting behavior will be purposeful and truthful. In life, people don't express themselves in a series of moments that flow effortlessly and seamlessly into each other, and when you see it in a performance, it always looks and sounds like acting. Let the person you are playing be a real person, living each moment as it comes. Wonderful, surprising things will happen.

■ *Why are the differences between "what" and "how" so important?*

The distinction between "what" and "how" is the difference between the character's approach to his own life and the way an actor might mistakenly deal with the same experiences *for* the character. It is an important distinction because actor decisions interfere, in every case, with the truthful behavior of the character. The character is only concerned with *what* he needs to do and *what* he needs to say in order to live his life.

To be truthful to that life, the actor must approach every moment and every word in the same way the character does. The actor must not decide *how* the character behaves and speaks. The character will do the behaving and speaking for himself as his life instructs him to do.

■ *What are "inner cues"?*

An "inner cue" is the character's specific thought that causes him to speak or to act. What is commonly thought of as a cue, something the character sees, hears, feels, tastes or smells, is not the thing that determines the nature of his reaction. It is his *perception* of that sensation that causes him to react. The same stimulus will cause different people to react in different ways (at different times) based on their own unique life experiences, even though all other factors seem to be the same.

In order to better understand the uniqueness of sense reactions in different people, observe two characters, Bill and Marie, together in the following situations:

1. They are in a movie theater and they see a tall, red-headed man buying popcorn.
    Marie is reminded of her brother whom she hasn't seen in two years.
    Bill is reminded of Marie's former boyfriend.

2. They are alone in their mountain cabin and they hear a gunshot.
    Marie is an avid skeet shooter and has been around guns all her life.
    Bill's brother was shot to death six weeks ago.

3. They are walking through a high-fashion department store and they see an elegant mink coat. They feel the texture of the coat.
    Marie recalls the coat that her father gave her mother on their anniversary.
    Bill recalls the television special he saw last night on the brutal trapping of fur-bearing animals.

4. They are in a restaurant, eating gumbo. They taste oysters.
    Marie really likes oysters.

In his college fraternity initiation, Bill had to eat 100 raw oysters in three minutes. He's never forgotten it.

5. They are at a dinner party and the host is wearing cologne.
    It is the same cologne Marie's father wore.
    It is the cologne the funeral director wore at Bill's sister's funeral.

Reactions to inner cues provide some of the most illuminating and surprising character moments, for actors as well as for audiences. The options are limitless. Take advantage of every opportunity to engage the character's senses. And don't predict what his reactions will be. Dare to be surprised.

■ *What is "privileged information"?*

"Privileged information" is information that the actor has, which the character must not have. The actor knows everything in the script. Much of that material provides vital clues to the actor's development of the character, but that same information might not be available to the character. For instance, several characters in the script might have conversations about your character's behavior or about the behavior of others toward your character, revealing important aspects of his personality and his essence. But your character might have no way of knowing that those things were said about him, so his feelings and behavior toward those characters cannot be influenced by the fact of their gossipy activities.

An actor has to be extremely protective of privileged information so that the information isn't used to *instruct* the character to behave untruthfully or uncharacteristically in a particular situation. The character never knows what comes next. Even though the actor knows how it will turn out, he has to resist the temptation to help the character through the difficult moments on his way to that cheerful (or not so cheerful) ending. The audience has paid for the privilege of experiencing all the moments with the character, and they should not be deprived of whatever might happen when the character is allowed to deal with them on his own.

Just such an opportunity occurred in the film *Out of Sight*. A small-time crook named Jack Foley, played by George Clooney (Supporting Actor Academy Award winner in *Syriana*), attempts a bank robbery. He instructs a teller to give him the money in her drawer if she doesn't want his accomplice, the man sitting with an open briefcase on the floor in front of the manager's desk, to shoot the manager, *even though Foley has no idea who the man is*. After presenting his note, Foley waits for the money, and never again, until he leaves, does he consider the man at the manager's desk. Foley gets the money and exits the bank. End of scene. No problem — a*nd no suspense.*

What George Clooney knew, and Jack Foley should not (and could not) have known, was that the man sitting with the open briefcase at the manager's desk wouldn't close the briefcase, get up, and leave the bank before the teller handed over the money. Consequently, Foley wasn't anxious, the scene had little tension, and the audience was denied the suspense and excitement that truthfulness would have provided. All because the character received privileged information, which caused him to behave in a manner inconsistent with the demands of truth.

In the case of the aforementioned scene in *Out of Sight*, it is possible that when the scene was shot, Jack Foley was truthfully and appropriately concerned about the geography of his clandestinely recruited partner, but, for any number of reasons, those moments may have been edited out. Ultimately, the actor is responsible for his own work, and he has to take it upon himself to pay careful attention to the details (even though what finally appears on the screen may have been out of his control). His reputation and the character's integrity depend on it.

■ *What do you mean by "natural sequence of behavior"?*

Human behavior (speech and action) happens in a natural sequence. That sequence is always the same. The event comes first. Then the character becomes involved. These are the steps that always occur:

1. An event happens.

2. The character sees, hears, feels, smells, tastes or senses the occurrence of the event (or the character is unaware of the event, in which case none of the following steps apply).

3. The character is affected by the information.

4. The character responds.

5. The character evaluates his response (and lets it stand or follows up with an additional response).

I offer the following three examples of sequential behavior:

1. A. A small child is in the path of a moving car.
    B. Character sees the child and the car.
    C. Character feels agitated by what he sees, and he is energized or immobilized (if he is immobilized, the following two steps don't apply).
    D. Character screams at the driver of the car.
    E. Character decides that the driver might not be able to hear him, so he runs toward the car (or the child).

2. A. First Character says, "Can we speak privately?"
    B. Second Character hears First Character ask for a private moment.
    C. Second Character feels uneasy, thinking that First Character's request portends something unpleasant.

      D. Second Character says "Can't we talk here?" First Character says, "I'd rather not."

      E. Second Character feels more uneasy, takes a deep breath and says, "Okay, I'll be right there" and walks into First Character's office.

3. A. It begins to rain.

     B. Character feels raindrops.

     C. Character looks up at the sky and assesses the probabilities of a heavy rain.

     D. Character walks to his front door, takes an umbrella off the bench, opens it and walks out into the rain.

     E. Character sticks out his hand to check the rain, considers the prospects for more rain and continues walking away from the house (or walks back into the house).

No matter how quickly the steps in the natural sequence of behavior occur, they always occur. Do not get ahead of the truth. Let the character work it out. When a character behaves truthfully, the actor disappears and the audience is engaged.

■ *Is there a difference between demonstrating and indicating?*

Yes. One is truthful and the other is not.

Indicating is *objective* acting. When an actor thinks a character should have a particular feeling (or lack of feeling), speak in a particular way or behave in a particular way, and then shows the audience what he thinks, he is indicating. Besides its usually evident falseness, indicating gets in the way of whatever might be occurring at that moment in the life of the character if the character were allowed to experience it. Indicating is sometimes called fake acting (because it is).

Demonstrating, because it is *subjective*, shows what the character is actually experiencing by allowing the character to experience it. Demonstrating is a vital part of the acting process. Regardless of the honesty of the actor's work, that work is essentially worthless if it all stays inside the character. Everything must be demonstrated *and communicated to the audience*, even a character's inability to express what he thinks and feels. Without the demonstration there is no performance.

■ *What does "permission" have to do with acting?*

Every person's behavior (including speech) has some relationship to the level of "permission" granted by the people with whom he interacts. Except for very young children, the mentally impaired and sociopaths, every person makes some adjustment in every situation based upon his assessment of the other people who are present. That aspect of character needs to be recognized and demonstrated for characters to be true to life.

The seeking and granting of permission is sometimes very subtle, but the process always happens. To illustrate this concept, I frequently ask actors if they ever speak to strangers on elevators. The answer to that question is usually, "Yes." Then I ask if they ever *don't* speak to strangers on elevators. The answer to that question is also usually, "Yes." The difference, of course, is that in some instances permission was granted and in other instances permission was withheld.

Permission is granted or withheld in the eyes and the body language — especially in the eyes. The eyes control the very first moment of communication between two people (unless for some reason the eyes can't be seen, as, for example, in a telephone conversation), and what is communicated in that first moment determines a great deal about how the relationship proceeds (or does not). Levels of trust, relative strength and compatibility can be established in that instant.

Real eye contact, which means *communicating* with the eyes, is an empowering aspect of acting which many actors neglect entirely, or try to fake with "meaningful" (meaningless) looks and glances. Honest eye contact initiated by one character has the power to improve all the acting in a scene, and, ultimately, in an entire production. The ability to establish that kind of visual contact is one of the defining qualities of a good actor.

Furthermore, an actor in an audition who allows his character to immediately contact the eyes of the other character (the reader) will draw that person into the scene and create unexpectedly truthful moments for himself and for everyone who is watching. I believe that that one ingredient can win an audition.

Actors need to take notice of the unspoken interaction that occurs between people in *all* real-life situations. In an acting situation, it is frequently those subtle, truthful interchanges that bring life to a performance and memorable moments to an audience.

■ *How important is the element of surprise, and how can I get that into my performance?*

The element of surprise in character study and in performance is not only very important, it is crucial to the truthfulness of the work. Surprises occur because of the ever presence of unpredictability in the character's life. If your life were a script, every page would be filled with revelations, and you would react appropriately, making adjustments all along the way. Some adjustments would be minor because the new information (*all information is new*, because the character either doesn't know about it or doesn't know precisely when or how it will be delivered) is either familiar or inconsequential. Some events, however, would be so unexpected that your programmed behavior would be disturbed.

In *Comes a Horseman*, my second film for director Alan J. Pakula, I play a geologist named George Bascomb, whose oilman boss, played by George Grizzard, wants drilling rights to property owned by two rival ranchers, played by Jane Fonda and Jason Robards. There is a scene in which I enthusiastically present my analysis and proposal to Jason Robards' character, and when I've finished, the script has George Grizzard's character dismissing me from the meeting with a simple, "Thank you."

In rehearsal, I mentioned to Alan that even though the script indicates that I leave the room, my character might not know that he's supposed to leave. Alan said, "Don't leave and let's see what happens." As the scene appears in the film, when George says, "Thank you," I sit down, proud and ready to participate in the rest of the meeting. Then George pointedly dismisses me, and to make sure I get it he says, "You can leave the plans here." So, I'm caught off guard. Embarrassed and feeling foolish, I get up and leave the room. The element of surprise reveals some nuances of my character and makes the moment very real.

Every script is filled with potential surprises. You will find them by being unprepared (as the character) for every new moment. Let the character's life be as difficult as it can be, even in the small details. Make him work to fulfill his life. Your acting will be much richer for it.

■ *What is memory of emotion, and what does it have to do with the actor's "comfort zone"?*

Emotional memory is the recollection and demonstration of feelings and behavior which occurred at some past time in the actor's life. It can be a helpful tool, in homework or class, for stretching the actor's emotional instrument. A character's feelings and behavior must not be subject to arbitrary limitations imposed by the actor's inability to fulfill the emotional demands of the role.

An actor's "comfort zone" may limit the actor's range of public expression to those forms of behavior that the actor finds personally comfortable, despite what a particular character requires. Truthful extremes of anger, sadness or joy are the least accessible feelings for many actors. Men, in particular, have been socialized out of certain kinds of emotional displays. An actor who finds himself too limited to draw the necessary emotion out of the script and demonstrate it needs to find another way to release the character's feelings. Recalling and reliving similar feelings from his own experience is one way of achieving that end.

Ideally, an actor will have recognized his emotional limitations, so those feelings will have been explored and released through study and homework before they need to be expressed on the job. Calling on emotional memory in the process of work on a particular role may result in reproducing the actor's real life moment instead of submitting to the character's moment.

I am opposed to the substitution of actor feelings for character feelings in actual rehearsal and performance because that process intrudes on the uniqueness of the character and eliminates any possibility of discovery and surprise.

Private emotional moments are usually more plentiful and much easier to recreate than public ones, so I suggest that you explore those memories. Moments of self-recrimination, resentment and imagined but unrealized confrontations are excellent sources for experiencing and demonstrating outward (but formerly private) manifestations of extreme sadness and anger. I also encourage you to make yourself very young in emotional exercises because childishness exposes the greatest extremes in feelings and behavior.

A good and plentiful source for emotional release exercises is available in many plays, movies and television shows. Actors should train themselves to be emotional audiences. Allowing one's self to *fully* respond to emotional stimuli in a darkened theatre or in the privacy of home is excellent practice in free outward expression of a complete range of feelings, from robust laughter to seething anger to unrestrained grief.

My own personal preference for the creation of emotional moments is for the actor to immerse himself in the life and condition of the character. Truthful character feelings will emerge on their own, often when the actor least expects them, and that phenomenon is one of acting's greatest rewards.

In order to illustrate the point that the script provides all the emotional source material the actor needs, I contrived a film scene with this narrative:

Ext. Family home on a quiet country road. Veranda.
Morning.

A LITTLE BOY, six years old, runs out of the house, followed by a COCKER SPANIEL PUPPY. The little boy and the puppy fly off the veranda into the yard. They are both as joyous as can be. The little boy chases the puppy. The puppy chases the little boy.

SFX: CAR ENGINE, FAINT AT FIRST, THEN LOUDER, PICKING UP SPEED.

The puppy continues to chase the little boy around the yard, until the little boy lets the puppy catch him. They are in love. The little boy pretends to wrestle with the puppy, then hugs and kisses him.

SFX: CAR ENGINE IS LOUDER. FASTER. CLOSER.

The little boy continues to hug and kiss the puppy. The puppy plants dozens of kisses on the little boy's face. The little boy loves it. Suddenly, the puppy breaks free and dashes toward the road and out of the frame.

Ext. Suburban country road. Morning.

SFX: CAR ENGINE IS LOUD. FAST. CLOSE.

A black Corvette speeds into the frame as the puppy runs into the road. The Corvette hits the puppy.

SFX: A SICKENING THUD.

> LITTLE BOY (V.O.)
> Nooooooo!

The Corvette speeds away. The little boy rushes to the puppy, but it is way too late. He kneels next to the lifeless little body, as tears stream down his face. He picks up the puppy, holds it in his lap, then hugs it, and kisses it and kisses it and kisses it…

> LITTLE BOY
> Nooooooo!

And the tears flow.

FADE OUT.

In the foregoing scene, the child actor playing the little boy is required to cry because the character cries. The character cries because the scene is very sad. The child actor cries for the same reason. And every member of the audience cries for the same reason. No member of the audience needs an emotional memory exercise recalling the death of a puppy in order to cry at this scene. Even those in the audience who never had a puppy will cry. Every audience member and the child actor get the tears from the same source – the script. The material always provides the necessary and correct emotional

stimulus. If it is there for the character, it is there for the actor —
always. The actor just has to find it and submit to it.

■ *Is there some technical way to express the meanings of the words?*

No. There is no *technical* approach that will satisfactorily express the
meanings of words in a truthful way. The best, most reliable, most
direct and most truthful way to verbalize meanings is to allow the
character to do it his way.

If you have correctly identified the essence of the character and
made a thorough investigation of his other attributes (by using the
Subjective Situation Perception outline), you will know how much
he means what he says in every situation, and you will be well on
your way to discovering how he says it.

When an actor speaks a word in a way that doesn't convey the
character's desire to have his true beliefs and feelings known, it is as
much a lie as if the character had lied.

For example, a person who is late for an appointment because he
overslept might say, "I'm sorry I'm late, but there was a terrible accident on the freeway." When you hear this explanation with no
imagery connected to the word "terrible" you probably know the person is lying, because the word was used to concoct an excuse, rather
than to express what the person actually saw. If the person had wit-
nessed the scene that prompted the use of the descriptive word "terrible," he would have instinctively chosen that word because he still
had the mental image of someone's arm lying on the freeway or some
other *terrible* sight, and you would know he was telling the truth.

If the actor plays a character who had actually driven past and wit-
nessed the accident scene, but he says "terrible" without that imagery, then he is falsifying his own work and making an inadvertent
liar out of the character.

There are at least eight categories of words to which actors need to pay *particular* attention, because characters choose those words, *often with opinions attached*, to convey important ideas. Seven of those categories include words (and phrases) that describe absolutes, extremes, unusual conditions or situations, qualities, quantities, horror and feelings.

Obvious words in those categories would include, respectively: "always," "none" and "best"; "tiny," "hot" and "most"; "quintuplets," "billionaire" and "amnesia"; "green," "thick" and "sluggish"; "ninety-nine," "bushel" and "furlong"; "decapitated," "entrails" and "bloody"; and "thrilling," "joyful" and "frightened." Less obvious are words and phrases that have special importance only because of the context, such as "barefoot" (on the streets of Chicago in January), "champagne" (in a concentration camp) or "pools" (of blood on the carpets and the furniture).

The eighth category is all verbs that describe *qualities* of thought, feelings or behavior, as in the following sentences: "I *ran* all the way"; "They *honored* me for my achievements"; "I *screamed* in pain"; "I *agonized* over it"; "She really *disgusts* me."

Beware of *inadvertent* double-talk. *Webster's Seventh New Collegiate Dictionary* offers this definition: "double-talk: language that appears to be earnest and meaningful but in fact is a mixture of sense and nonsense." The great television comedian Sid Caesar is a master of double-talk in many languages. He can't speak the languages, but he knows exactly how they sound. When the Italians and the French hear his hilarious routines, it drives them crazy because it sounds to them as if he is speaking their languages *perfectly* but they can't understand a word of it, unless he inserts a real word for comic effect (anyone who isn't familiar with the genius of Sid Caesar should buy or rent a video entitled *Ten from "Your Show of Shows"*). The nightclub and television comedian Norm Crosby has built an entire career on a masterful misuse of the English language.

For both Sid and Norm, double-talk is the basis and the intent for the work. Unfortunately, many actors inadvertently fill their performances with double-talk, effectively cheating the work out of its deserved impact. When an actor fails to use words as the character clearly intends for them to be used, he is engaging in double-talk. If the actor double-talks convincingly, it will sound like he is speaking in a truthful way, even though he has conveyed very little truthfulness.

Actors should observe the way children express themselves as a guide to finding important words and truthfully communicating their meanings. Children are very good at making their intentions known. A child who isn't allowed to go outside after dinner says, "You NEVER let me go out after dinner." If you have something a child desires, that desire is expressed in no uncertain terms. "I WANT it."

In life, people get the point across perfectly when they intend to be understood. Every character will behave in the same way, unless the actor prevents it. When a character is denied the full meaning of the words he chooses to express himself, the actor appears to have learned English phonetically without having been told what he is talking about.

If you ever need to speak in a *foreign* language with which you are unfamiliar, you have two tasks. First, you obviously have to learn to pronounce the words exactly as the character pronounces them. Just as important, however, is your need to know what each word means so that the character can effectively and truthfully say it the way he means it.

Situations calling for actors to speak some lines in foreign languages come up more often than you might think. Academy Award-winning director Mel Gibson (*Braveheart*) shot his acclaimed and controversial *The Passion of the Christ* entirely in Aramaic, Latin and Hebrew.

On the set of *The Ice Runner* in Moscow, during a break in the shooting, I attempted to have a conversation with one of the Soviet actors, but he had no idea what I was saying. He was acting in English, but he couldn't speak English. He had learned to *pronounce* the English words, and he learned what the words meant in Russian in order to act the part. If he hadn't known *precisely* what he was saying and spoken the words to that effect, his performance would have suffered considerably. His extra effort paid off to the extent that no one who sees the performance would know what the actor went through to achieve it.

■ *What is subtext, and what do you mean when you say, "Let the subtext write the text"?*

Subtext is what the character is thinking at all times, when he is speaking and when he is silent. The character is always thinking about something, because he always has something to think about. It is what human beings do all the time.

In real life, however, we are free to allow our minds to wander. When we act, we have no such luxury, even when the character (like Walter Mitty, played by the great Danny Kaye, in the film *The Secret Life of Walter Mitty*) daydreams, because, even then, the daydreams are specific. The character's thoughts need to be appropriate to the material of the script and they need to be constant.

Beware of random thoughts, even though they may be character thoughts, that have nothing to do with the character's life in the context of the script. Not only will the resulting behavior (facial expressions, vocal inflections, etc.) be confusing, an opportunity for the character to illuminate some aspect of the story will have been squandered.

Carefully focused, uncomplicated subtext brings characters to life, resulting in behavior that is not only recognizably human and truthful, but is also clear and understandable, *even though the audience's understanding of the behavior may not become fully enlightened until subsequent events unfold.* A character's words are usually determined by current events, even though his thoughts and feelings may be in memories and anticipation of other occurrences. But those past or future events must at some point be revealed to the audience. Otherwise, the behavior will be confusing at best and sleep-inducing at worst.

Christopher Walken (who won the Academy Award for Best Supporting Actor in *The Deer Hunter*) is one of the most consistently interesting (and employed) actors with whom I have worked (*The Milagro Beanfield War* and *Communion*). In interviews about his acting, he has frequently referred to subtext as something to which he gives great attention as a constant vital ingredient in his work. It adds dimension to every character he plays, as it will for every actor who gives his characters the freedom to think.

The word "subtext" implies that it is underneath the text, as character thoughts and feelings that might not be spoken — and so it is. But subtext is also the source of what *is* spoken. In reality, subtext should be called *sourcetext*, because it is the character's thoughts that *cause* him to speak or determine *how* he speaks (or refrains from speaking or behaves in any other way). In that sense, the subtext writes the text, and any other motivation for the character's speech and actions would be based on something the actor decides, as if the actor had hypnotized the character into behaving against his will.

Allow the character to find his own appropriate thoughts and think them, and all of his behavior will emerge from those thoughts. Beyond enriching your work beyond measure, the use of subtext will free you from the need to fill your character's moments with acting stuff (never a good idea).

▪ *What is the "point" of a line of dialogue?*

The "point" of a line of dialogue is the *character's intention* in that line—the meaning behind the words and, especially, his *reason* for choosing those particular words (and his reason for choosing to speak at all).

Characters in a script behave like real people, and real people frequently don't say *exactly* what they mean every time they speak. The dynamics of the situation (Subjective Situation Perception) govern a character's intent in expressing himself. The ability or desire of a character to say (or not say) what he really means is an important ingredient and indicator of the character's essence.

To find the point of a line, *paraphrase it as concisely as possible from what is actually on the character's mind at that moment*, regardless of the words he actually uses. Identifying that *idea* will guide you to the point of the line. Here are two examples:

1. The line reads:

   "We have a lot of ground to cover, and enemy infantry is all around us. They are the best marksmen in Europe."

   But the point of the line is:

   "Don't do anything stupid to get us killed."

2. The line reads:

   "I'm really looking forward to your move, Mom, and I know you'll be able to make new friends here."

   But the point of the line may be:

   "If you move here, it will interfere with my privacy and my social life."

By getting to the point of the line, you eliminate all temptation to merely report the written information that may actually obscure the character's intent. The moment then reveals what is really going on in the character's mind. Once you understand the point of the line, the scripted words will communicate the character's thoughts and feelings (insofar as the character wants them communicated).

Words and phrases can have multiple meanings, and those words and phrases will sound very different, depending on which meaning the character has attached to them. Never take the words at face value. The character's words are not a news story, and the actor is not a reporter. I offer the following example of a common phrase with many meanings. The character says:

"I love you."

The point of the line may be any one of the following:

1. "I want to make love to you."
2. "I *need* you sexually."
3. "You are a wonderful person."
4. "We have a special bond of friendship (or family)."
5. "I want you to be my romantic partner for the rest of my life."
6. "I want you to be my romantic partner for the rest of the night."
7. "I am so needy and possessive that if you leave me, I will kill myself."
8. "I am so needy and possessive that if you leave me, I will kill you."
9. "I really respect you, but I'm not *in love* with you."
10. "I want you to believe that I have special feelings for you (because I want something from you, but I don't particularly care about you at all)."

Even though a character's verbal responses to any given situation may seem spontaneous, they are never random. Even when a character speaks glibly and apparently carelessly, he *chooses* his words. The choice of words and the thought process that determines the choice are important aspects of character. Finding the character's specificity in all his behavior will excite you as an actor and will bring your work to life.

■ *What is a "thought pause"?*

A "thought pause" is a brief, natural interruption in speech caused by the character's momentary inability to form or complete a thought. While these pauses frequently occur as interruptions of single thoughts, they also happen between thoughts.

An example of a necessary thought pause in the midst of a single thought would be in this line of dialogue, which, as written, says:

"What's happening to me is so intense that it's ninety-five percent more serious than anything in your pathetic life."

Spoken as written, the line would imply that the character had the "ninety-five" preprogrammed in his head, just waiting to be released. But the fact is that he had to come up with that number, instead of, say, "seventy-five" or "eighty" or "ninety-eight" or "a hundred." But he didn't choose those other numbers. He chose "ninety-five." In the piece of a moment in which that numerical selection is made, there is some pause, the extent of which would be determined by the character of the speaker. The character's selection of the word "pathetic" (instead of "meaningless," "pitiful," "unfortunate," etc.) might receive the same treatment. So the line could actually be written (and spoken) as:

"What's happening to me is so intense that it's…ninety-five percent more serious than anything in your pathetic life."

or as:

"What's happening to me is so intense that it's…ninety-five percent more serious than anything in your…pathetic life."

Of course, the character might give the same consideration to the word "intense" or the word "serious" and on and on.

Without the natural choppiness of truthful speech, acting always sounds like acting, because the actor, unlike the character, always knows what comes next. Pauses *between* thoughts also occur naturally in human speech, but seldom in acting speech. The best and most well-known example of pauses between thoughts happens repeatedly in the long-running series of *Columbo* television movies. In every installment of the series, Columbo (as played brilliantly by

Peter Falk) comes up with a clever deduction with which he torments the killer. As written, it might look like this:

> COLUMBO
>
> Thanks for your help, doctor. Here's my card. If you think of anything else, please call me. Oh, by the way, one more thing. You said your wife got home at six o'clock. But you didn't arrive until seven. How did you know she was there at six?

But Columbo pauses between thoughts. In fact, he pauses so long that he has time to leave the room and come back to express the next thought. So, in order to accommodate Columbo's action, the dialogue would have to be written like this:

> COLUMBO
>
> Thanks for your help, doctor. Here's my card. If you think of anything else, please call me.

Columbo leaves the room.

Columbo comes back into the room.

> COLUMBO
>
> Oh, by the way, one more thing. You said your wife got home at six o'clock. But you didn't arrive until seven. How did you know she was there at six?

Character and situation determine the occurrence and the nature of thought pauses. Only the most impulsive or dishonest character would never experience thought pauses. When it happens, it is only because the character hasn't completed his thought for that brief, perhaps barely perceptible moment. It should never happen because the actor decides that it's a good place to pause. That would be one of those actor decisions that creates an obviously false moment.

■ *What is "vocality" of character?*

I use the word "vocality" to refer to the five categories of speech that affect the way a character expresses himself verbally. Each category demonstrates a different aspect of speech. When they are put together, they produce the character's unique voice and reveal important information about that character's essence and life.

The most basic attribute of speech is the tone or the depth of sound of the voice. The pitch of the human voice provides the first impression of a person's relative strength and authority. Stereotypically, the deeper the voice, the more authoritative and powerful the person is perceived to be. Conversely, generally speaking, a high-pitched voice wouldn't immediately inspire confidence in that person's capacity to lead and command. Despite the fact that there have been notable exceptions like James Cagney (Academy Award-winning actor in *Yankee Doodle Dandy*) and Marlon Brando, leading men are expected to have deep voices. But, as in the cases of Cagney and Brando, force of character can make an intrinsically average-seeming, or high- pitched voice quite commanding enough.

For women, childlike, thin or squeaky voices aren't indicative of dominant personalities. An actress whose everyday speech falls into any of those categories, in a character with a forceful nature, will, generally speaking, need to surrender those tendencies to the demands of the character.

The second attribute is refinement or precision of pronunciation. The clarity with which a person speaks is indicative of his intelligence, education and social class. The greater the clarity, the smarter, better educated and higher class a person would appear to be. However, *exaggerated* clarity might suggest someone of very limited or even retarded intellectual capacity struggling to reproduce or repeat the words precisely as he had memorized them. Academy Award-winning characterizations by Cliff Robertson in *Charly*, Dustin Hoffman in *Rain Man* and Tom Hanks in *Forrest Gump* utilized this attribute to demonstrate retardation, as did Peter Sellers' brilliant performance in *Being There*. Mumbled or impeded speech is associated with uneducated lower classes, although some speech impediments are merely physical challenges.

The third attribute is tempo. A slow or interrupted rate of speech would tend to indicate that the speaker is thoughtful or cautious, but it might signal dull-wittedness or insecurity. A fast talker is likely to be quick-witted, impulsive or infused with nervous energy. Obviously, speed of speech can be affected by age, health or medication.

The fourth attribute of speech is purity of sound. Most people speak in relatively unblemished tones, and because their sound is somewhat ordinary, those voices are also uninteresting. Exceptionally resonant or melodic, as well as nasal, raspy, guttural and breathy voices tend to capture more attention because they are unusual.

The fifth attribute is dialect or accent. In addition to the nation or region of a person's upbringing, the accent sometimes reveals the place or the ethnicity of the neighborhood in which he grew up, overshadowing more important aspects of character. The well-known Massachusetts political family, the Kennedys, for example, despite their wealth, education and sophistication, speak in a decidedly lower class dialect, revealing a more recent entry into the social position of local long-established families of privilege.

Characters do express all aspects of their vocality, if the actor's instrument is sufficiently free to respond to the information and the instruction that the character provides. I suggest that actors allow their vocal instruments to perform what is within their normal range of sounds, rather than forcing something false or unsustainable out of themselves.

When Academy Award-winning actor Sir Laurence Olivier (*Hamlet*), then in his late fifties, played Othello, he used a deeper sound than he had ever used before, because he believed the character required it. The result was quite effective and natural sounding at the deep end of Olivier's normal speaking range, but it would have been bizarre if he had attempted to create basso sounds from his high baritone voice.

In the matter of accents, an actor who doesn't have a gifted ear would do well to take great care, with or without the help of a dialect coach, to faithfully and naturally speak the speech of the character. The best sources of authentic accents are through personal contacts or recordings of English language speeches, interviews and conversations with actual native speakers from the place where the character learned to speak. Research the experience and the industry reputation of prospective dialect coaches to assure yourself that what you will get is the real thing.

Actors should reject the temptation to use the voice in ways that are not organically connected to the character. In particular, phony vocal "styles" associated with "classical acting," especially in Shakespeare, should be avoided.

My friend Herbert Rudley, an excellent, very truthful actor with many important roles on the New York stage and in films and television, recalls an experience he had in the Broadway production of *Macbeth* with the renowned British stars Maurice Evans and Dame Judith Anderson. Evans was concerned that Herb, who was playing Macduff, might have vocal problems over the long run, playing the role as fully (and honestly) as he had begun to play it. "Oh, no, dear boy, your voice will never last," Evans cautioned. "You might want to use my technique. In the dramatic scenes, I always begin at middle C, la la la, and then up the scale, la la la, as the scene builds. It saves the voice." Fortunately for Herb, he never took the advice.

It is interesting to note that when the great British stage director Sir Tyrone Guthrie was asked to categorize the notable Hamlets he had seen, he said, "John Gielgud was the most poetic (and the best), Laurence Olivier was the most athletic, John Barrymore was the most romantic and Maurice Evans was the most consistently audi-ble." Audibility is not the quality for which an actor wants to be best remembered.

■ *What do you mean when you say, "Forget the words"?*

Memorizing the words is critical to the actor's ability to play a role because without the character's *specific* words we have no way to understand the important verbal part of his communication. But the character doesn't know the words in advance. He dreams them up as the need arises.

The actor must not *plan* to say what the character hasn't planned to say. For that reason, the actor has to forget the words until the character selects them and speaks them. Thoughts always precede the words. The actor has to "unwrite" the script – then think the thoughts that cause him to speak.

■ *What is phrasing?*

Phrasing is verbal punctuation. Written punctuation is used to gram-matically clarify the meaning of a line of dialogue. Because laws of punctuation serve a strictly literary function, however, they cannot be relied upon to accommodate a character's thoughts and feelings when *speaking* the line. Phrasing is the mental and verbal technique that characters use to express themselves. Sometimes even a very short sentence may be phrased differently by different characters in different situations. For example, the sentence "I don't know" can be phrased in *at least* five different ways:

1. "I don't know."

When spoken in this way, the character expresses certainty. He is sure that he doesn't know, or he wants the listener to believe he is sure that he doesn't know.

2. "I…don't know."

This phrasing suggests that the character has been surprised or is trying to think of (or make up) an answer.

3. "I don't…know."

In this example, the character's original intention was to say something else. It might have been something like, "I don't think it matters." But, whatever it was, he stopped in mid-sentence to reconsider his response.

4. "I…don't…know."

This phrasing expresses utter confusion. Any more confusion than this would likely be expressed by stammering or speechlessness.

5. "I don't know…"

This seemingly incomplete expression is actually quite complete. Phrasing the line in this way, the character is actually saying, "I don't know what to say."

The foregoing illustration is only an example of the almost infinite possibilities inherent in even the *seemingly* least significant piece of material. Don't preconceive and don't limit the possibilities of language. *Let the character speak*, and allow yourself to be surprised by *how* he says what he has to say.

■ *What is grouping?*

Grouping is the connecting of two or more sentences into a single, seemingly uninterrupted speech flow. Sentences are so grouped in speech (if not in punctuation) for two reasons. First, the thoughts are connected in such a way that to speak them with an interrupting pause would defy logic. Second, the human ear is so attuned to these natural connections in normal speech that to disconnect them creates an impression of falseness or contrivance ("acting" to create some effect). Here are two examples of sentences that need to be grouped:

1. "You hit him in the face. Why did you do that?"

2. "They both arrived late. Barry's plane was grounded in Berlin. Sybil didn't get the message until Tuesday."

In each of the foregoing examples, pausing between the sentences would lose both the logic and the impulse of the moment.

Sometimes, however, truthfulness demands a very different kind of grouping. In Academy Award-winning best picture *On the Water-front*, directed by the great Elia Kazan (Academy Award winner), Terry Malloy, played by Marlon Brando (Academy Award winner), has a memorable scene in a taxicab with his brother Charley, played by Rod Steiger. In that scene, Terry has a short monologue, which includes a sequence of four sentences, that illustrates the power of truthful grouping. Terry says:

"I coulda been a contenda. I coulda been somebody. Instead of a bum. Which is what I am."

Brando separates the sentences into three groups thus:

"I coulda been a contenda. I coulda been somebody. [pause] Instead of a bum. [pause] Which is what I am."

Brando's truthful grouping in that brief moment makes an impact that is almost heartbreaking.

■ *What is a beat?*

A beat, in directing and acting terminology, means two different things, depending on the context.

When referring to time, a beat is a short (usually a second or two) pause between acting moments. The expression is thought to have originated when a German director in Hollywood once referred to a "bit" (which sounded like "beat") of time that he wanted to lapse before the actor spoke his next line or initiated a new piece of action. The term sounds a little mechanical to me, so I prefer to use the word "moment."

There are also dramatic beats. In this context, a beat is a change of intention or a new impulse that occurs within a scene, so that a director might instruct the actor that "this is a new beat," meaning that the character's feelings or behavior change in some way. The beat can change even within a single sentence, as in this example:

"I really love you, [new beat] but if you betray me, I'll kill you."

Beats in this context are necessary, truthful expressions of changes in feelings and behavior and, consequently, provide extremely effective dramatic moments. Without dramatic beats, the energy of real life would be missing.

■ *What are obstacles and what is their importance?*

An obstacle is an impediment or restraint that inhibits a character's behavior and prevents him from proceeding toward some desired goal. A character's essence is often best demonstrated by his reaction to obstacles. Obstacles are important because they are essential elements of reality. A character who never encountered obstacles would be a character without real life experiences.

Character obstacles fall into two categories: mental and physical.

The mental obstacle, or obstacle of thought, is that barrier created in the mind of the character which prevents the fulfillment of some task, even though the character is physically able to perform the task. For example:

The character is in serious financial distress. He expects to hear from one of his creditors, but he has no way to pay the bill, no way to explain his delinquency, and no way to get the money.

The telephone rings.

The character stares at the ringing telephone, but fear prevents him from picking up the receiver. Fear is the mental obstacle. Except for the fear, the character is physically capable of answering the phone.

The second category of obstacles is the physical obstacle, or obstacle of action, in which the character is physically restrained from performing a task, even though he desires to perform the task. For example:

The character arrives home just in time to receive an important, long-awaited phone call from her boyfriend. As she arrives at the door to her apartment:

The telephone rings.

She reaches into her purse for her key, but can't find it. She checks all her pockets, but still can't find the key. She tries the door, but it is securely locked. The locked door is the physical obstacle. The character wants, maybe even needs to get inside the apartment to answer the phone, but is physically prevented from doing so.

Every life is *filled* with obstacles. The more challenging the obstacles, the more interesting the character. The obstacles are there. Find them and make the character deal with them.

■ *What is the meaning and the importance of conflict?*

As I use the term, conflict is any opposition by another character (seen or unseen) that would prevent (by intention or otherwise) your character's achievement of his purpose. Conflict is also your character's opposition to prevent another character from achieving his purpose.

It is important for actors to identify conflicts, because, much like obstacles, they are the engine that drives all dramatic (tragic and comic) literature. Without conflicts and obstacles, no novel would be readable and no play, theatrical film or television drama (or comedy) would be watchable. *Your character experiences conflicts. Find them.*

■ *What is "programmed behavior"?*

"Programmed behavior" is the expression I use to describe the many expressions, comments, statements, announcements and responses that people make *automatically* every day, without much, if any, forethought.

Although each individual has his own collection of favorites, some of the most common expressions are greetings and their responses, such as, "How are you, today?" "I'm just great. How are you?" "What a pretty dress." "Is it hot enough for you?" "Where have you been lately?" and "What's new?" Sometimes programmed behavior is sincere. Sometimes it is not. But it is always relatively routine.

The importance of programmed behavior is not its ordinariness, but its contrast with unusual or unexpected behavior. People engage in and respond to expected behavior and events rather smoothly, but anything unforeseen is startling to some degree, and the regularly scheduled, programmed behavior never happens. A character's truthful, surprised reaction to the unexpected is a necessary and often neglected aspect of the actor's work. Unpredictable events cause unpredictable responses. *You cannot plan unpredictable behavior. It just happens.*

Here are two examples of unexpected occurrences that prevent programmed responses:

1. *Oscar*: Hey, man, it's good to see you. How're you doing?
    Jack: Not too good. They fired me.

Whatever Oscar's ordinary and anticipated conversation might have been, all the dynamics have been altered while he adjusts to what he has just heard. *Regardless of the scripted response, Oscar cannot speak until he has processed the surprising information.* The nature of his response will depend on the essence of his character and his relationship to Jack.

2. *Sylvia*: What took you so long? Where's Billy?
    Melanie: I've just spent three hours in the police station. He's been kidnapped.

Sylvia is shocked. Whatever she expected to hear, this isn't it. And there will be no programmed response. She can't speak until she recovers from the shock. Sylvia's character and her relationships to Melanie and Billy will govern her reaction to the news, but no words or actions will come until the moment of shock has passed. Even though that moment may be quite short, *the moment must occur. Otherwise, the moments that follow will be false and will appear false.*

■ *What is the "tone" of a script, and how should that affect my approach to the work?*

The "tone" of a script is the style of the material and the approach to the material that are intended by the writer and the director. Melodramatic, farcical, theatrical, naturalistic, documentary and Amplified Realism are examples of tone. With the exception of Amplified

Realism and documentary, they each offer a distorted approach to truthfulness. Consequently, the tone of a project also determines its believability. Sometimes the writer and the director are aware of the level of believability they have achieved, but sometimes they are not.

Your goal as an actor is always truthfulness of character, so your character will always be believable, regardless of the universe in which he lives. However, the character has to belong in that universe. For example, in a farcical universe, even though the events are farcical, the characters believe the events to be real. Therefore, your character must do whatever is necessary to behave truthfully and communicate believably with the other characters; his *perception* of them and of everything else in his universe will determine how he does that. You must not force the issue of tone on the character. Trust the character to take care of it.

■ *What is the difference between naturalism and truthfulness?*

Naturalism is objective. An actor who strives to be naturalistic would have to observe real or natural human behavior and then attempt to reproduce it as stylistically accurate as possible. A naturalistic character would be a copy of a real person (or of someone else's performance). He seems almost lifelike, but lacks *specific* truthfulness. This interesting observation was made in Marlon Brando's obituary in *Variety* (July12-18, 2004), contrasting Brando's work to a kind of acting that preceded him: "Even with naturalistic film actors, audiences knew they were watching rehearsed make-believe." Yes, if that was what the audiences were watching, they certainly knew it.

Of course, there were truthful (and interesting) actors before Marlon Brando. But in his best moments, and there were a lot of them, he was a great one.

Truthfulness is subjective. The actor whose goal is truthfulness studies his character and allows the character to be the source of his own existence. The character is alive and real. He is an original.

■ When you discuss "purpose," do you really mean "objective"?

No. I use the word "purpose" because it *doesn't* have the same meanings as the word "objective."

In one sense, objective and purpose have similar meanings because they both demand an answer to the question, "What do you want?" The critical difference for me is that the word objective doesn't seem to address the question, "Why do you want it?" *Every character always has a reason, or purpose, for desiring that particular result, and it is that reason that drives him toward his goal. Purpose carries the strong implication of necessity, or need, which objective does not.* In fact, the character's needfulness of purpose, or the absence of that needfulness, might be the difference between a performance that the audience *needs* to see and one that they might just as well do without.

There is another striking difference between objective and purpose that makes me wonder how the word objective ever got into the acting lexicon. The second meaning of objective is, according to *Webster's New Collegiate Dictionary*, "Expressing or involving the use of facts without distortion by personal feelings or prejudices," a perfect definition of what acting is *not. There are no facts in acting except those that are distorted by the character's personal feelings and prejudices.* Additionally, the alternate meaning for purpose, also according to Webster's, is "determination." Of course, every actor must be determined and purposeful in demonstrating the character.

There are three levels of purpose, and that differentiation is an important aspect of character truthfulness. Every character has a *life* purpose, more comprehensive than the purpose that motivates his appearance in the script. The script (and, especially, the reason for the character's inclusion in it) provides the character's *dramatic* purpose. And each scene in which the character appears supplies an *immediate* purpose. It is important to note that the character's *action* in fulfilling his immediate purpose in a particular (possibly minor) scene, seemingly having nothing to do with his dramatic purpose, might actually illuminate his behavior that occurs in other, more pivotal scenes.

The initial task of clarifying character purpose rests with the writer. Nevertheless, the ultimate responsibility for demonstrating purpose at all times belongs to the actor, because the actor will get the credit or the blame for it. Whenever the character is allowed to behave truthfully, his purpose will always be clear. However, some scripts don't provide that clarity and, when they don't, the actors have to make it work.

In *Leaving Las Vegas*, Nicolas Cage (Academy Award winner) perfectly demonstrated the essence and purpose of a man bound for suicide by alcohol consumption. Without Cage's splendid performance, the film would have become very uninteresting very quickly because the character never wavered in his relentless descent, from moment to moment, from scene to scene, from ominous beginning to predictable end. Even though the story lacked texture, Nicolas Cage's performance was flawless, and it made the film watchable.

Mystic River is a film that presented a different kind of problem for the actors. Sean Penn's Academy Award-winning performance of the obsessively vengeful Jimmy Markum had to overcome that script's abandonment of Markum's need (purpose) to avenge his daughter's brutal murder *at the very moment that the killers' identities were revealed.*

By the end of *Mystic River*, two other excellent actors found their characters similarly derailed, but apparently completely ignored the scripted inconsistencies (and did it so well that they almost made the audience disregard the characters' forgetfulness of purpose). At the end of the picture, the dedicated cop, played by Kevin Bacon, suddenly, inexplicably deserts his job (purpose), to shift his attention to some part of his personal life that had nothing to do with the rest of the film. Marcia Gay Harden (Academy Award winner in *Pollock*) spends much of the film protecting husband Tim Robbins (whose very fine performance earned him the Best Supporting Actor Academy Award) from the police, then betrays him to the one person who will surely kill him. The plot was satisfied, but her character's purpose was not.

The acclaim that each of the aforementioned exceptional performances received is a testament to the importance of actors' uncompromising, uncritical acceptance of the scripts they are given to work with. It is only fair to mention that, my own tastes and judgments notwithstanding, both *Leaving Las Vegas* and *Mystic River* received widespread critical, public and industry adulation for acting, directing and writing.

Writers and actors need to be faithful to the characters they create and to make the characters' lives interesting. Character must be driven by the demands of the character's life instead of an arbitrary desire for dramatic effect. Nothing is so effective as uncompromised truthfulness. However, even when the writing doesn't provide those glorious, truthful moments, the actor has to find them. For the actor, it is always the best script ever written.

■ *What does reporting have to do with acting?*

Reporting is the reading or recitation of information without interpretation. A report contains no feeling. Nevertheless, a properly delivered report is a clear explanation of the material, which requires thought and understanding. A badly delivered report (which includes most radio and television news reports and many radio commercials, including some dramatized commercials) contains neither feeling nor thinking, only talking.

Reporting, even good reporting, has nothing to do with acting. Reporting is sometimes mistaken for acting, but only by actors, never by audiences.

■ *You say listening is important. Is there some special way to listen?*

You bet there is — and there is also a way *not* to listen.

Do not listen as an actor. The actor, as an impersonal participant in the situation, must not base his responses to audible stimuli on his objective opinion of what those responses ought to be. The objective analysis will turn itself into an objective (indicated) performance. When a character speaks as though he hasn't processed the preceding moment, you may be sure that the actor planned the response before the need to speak ever entered the character's experience. *That false moment will be detected by every member of the audience who is actually paying attention.*

Because so much of the character's feelings and behavior result from what the character hears, the actor needs to remove himself from the listening process and guard against his own natural (or contrived) reactions to *all sounds* in a script. The character may be unaware of the sound, even though the actor and the audience hear it. Conversely, the character might hear sounds that the actor and the audience can't hear, as Audrey Hepburn's blind character in *Wait Until Dark* was able to hear Jack Weston's character wiping fingerprints off the refrigerator and the staircase banister.

When the actor allows the *character* to listen, the character will subjectively behave appropriately and spontaneously. The character's feelings and thoughts will determine his unplanned and truthful responses. The character will relieve the actor of any responsibility for inventing line readings or "naturalistic" facial expressions and gestures. *The character's response must sound like he has heard and processed the sound (a human utterance or anything else) that engen-*

ders the response. The character *is*, and the actor would be well advised not to interfere with that.

■ *What does the word "compass" mean when you use it in discussing a role or a performance?*

I have adopted the word "compass" in discussing character because it has two meanings that relate perfectly to character development, completeness and direction. The industry uses the word "arc" to describe the same thing (and also many other things, also inappropriately), but, of course, it doesn't. In fact, an arc is part of a circle, incomplete and indefinite, two qualities that bear no relationship whatsoever to the craft of acting.

A compass contains all 360 degrees of a circle, complete, with nothing left out. Just as the compass is complete, so is every character complete. It is the actor's job to find all the parts. Unfortunately, it is a task without end. An actor must never be content with his discoveries of character (except, of course, that time constraints do force finalization for audition and performance purposes), because the content of every character is too vast to ever be revealed in its entirety. Fortunately, however, correct character work (like the compass) will point the actor in the *direction* of completeness.

Every actor (and every teacher and every coach) should strive to discover and demonstrate the completeness of character, even though the goal is unattainable. There is immense joy to be realized with every revelation of truth, and the accumulation of those moments provides the greatest rewards in acting.

■ *Do you recommend any specific acting exercises?*

In addition to study techniques suggested elsewhere in this book, there are six exercises I recommend as good reminders and reinforcement for truthful behavior. Consider the following:

1. Environment.

   Examine *all* of the actual elements in a room (or outdoor space), including other people, furniture and props and imagine them to be or to represent something different to your character, for *specific* attributes in the following categories:

   a. Familiar or *unfamiliar*.

   b. Pleasant or *unpleasant*.

   c. Safe or *dangerous*.

In each of the foregoing examples, pay particular attention to the many possibilities of the second alternative, because the problems suggested by those options will reveal the most interesting aspects of character. The character has feelings about his environment. Allow those feelings to emerge. Always be specific in choices of character and environment.

2. Actor Playwright.

   a. Select and memorize a monologue.

   b. Develop and rehearse the monologue, using all seven elements of Subjective Situation Perception as they relate to the actual circumstances in the script.

   c. Reconstruct the character's circumstances (except for the dialogue, which remains the same).

   d. Develop and rehearse the monologue, using all seven elements of Subjective Situation Perception as they relate to the new information.

   e. Repeat c and d. You can repeat this step an infinite number of times. There is no limit to the possibilities.

3. Feeling the News.

   a. Select a *news* article from a news magazine or newspaper.

   b. Choose a character (based on an essence that you select) to read the article aloud.

   c. Choose one general feeling that will affect the character as he reads the article.

    d. Choose the character to whom you are reading, with particular attention to his relationship to your character and your character's reason for choosing this person to read to at this particular time.

    e. Read the article aloud, making your character's relationship to each specific person and event in the article reinforce the general feeling.

    f. Change the character or the feeling (or both) and repeat the exercise. The possibilities of this exercise are endless.

4. Observing Reality.

The purpose of this exercise is for attuning the actor to the recognition and understanding of real human behavior, not for cataloging specific details to be reproduced or copied.

    a. Choose a person to observe.

Large public areas such as crowded restaurants and airport terminals are excellent locales for this exercise. Churches, hospital waiting rooms and other intimate settings are good subject sources to observe how people speak in those milieus, where behavior tends to be artificially toned down. *First-time* television or filmed documentary interviews with real people arc also good sources of truthful behavior (repetitive interviews with the same subject lose spontaneity as the interviewee becomes rehearsed in his responses). Politicians, professional actors and other celebrities (and public figures) are interesting subjects, but their speech and other behavior are specific to their particular spheres of notoriety and are highly unlikely to be truthful in any general way.

    b. Listen to the speech.

Pay particular attention to the person's choice of words that express absolutes, extremes, unusual concepts, quantities, qualities, strong emotions, horror and verbs that describe a *quality* of action. Listen for the special way that the person speaks those words.

   c. Describe the essence of that person's character.

   d. Imagine the person's subtext in the course of the conversation.

   e. Observe the person's body language (if you can do it unobtrusively).

5. Reading off the Page.

This is a good cold reading exercise in addition to providing a worthwhile means of isolating the character's *moment-by-moment* speech and other behavior. This approach can be used in preparing cold readings, as well as for memorizing lines.

   a. Choose a scene in which the character you will play has most of the dialogue (since the dialogue you speak is the basis of this exercise).

   b. Determine and describe your character's essence.

   c. Establish your character's feelings and his purpose for being in the scene.

   d. Use eye contact and body language to establish your character's relationship with the other character(s) in the scene.

   e. Look at the script and assimilate the words and the feelings that express the character's first idea.

   f. Look up and tell the idea (using the character's words) to the appropriate character.

   g. Look at the script and get the next idea.

   h. Listen (mentally) and react to the other characters' responses, *but don't anticipate them.* And don't anticipate the other characters' *non-responses.* For example, if you ask a question, expect an answer, even though the script tells you that no reply will be forthcoming. Remember, the character hasn't read the script.

    i. Repeat steps g, f and h throughout the scene.

    j. Repeat steps e through g, constantly increasing the number of ideas you absorb each time you refer to the script.

    k. Repeat steps e through g until you have memorized the scene.

6. Meaning (and Feeling) What You Say.

Words express ideas and feelings. Ideas that have different meanings and feelings shouldn't sound as if they feel the same and mean the same thing. Choose a series of adjectives that describe a person or thing, then speak them, expressing those meanings and feelings that cause the character to choose those words. For example:

Mary is lovable.

Mary is hateful.

Mary is gorgeous.

Mary is grotesque.

Mary is wealthy.

Mary is bankrupt.

Mary is funny.

Mary is humorless.

Mary is kind.

Mary is mean.

Mary is vigorous.

Mary is ill.

Mary is old.

Mary is youthful.

Mary is brilliant.

Mary is stupid.

Mary is fat.

Mary is skinny.

Mary is clever.

Mary is foolish.

The list of descriptive adjectives (and the various thoughts and feelings that cause those words to be spoken) that may be applied to a person or a thing is vast. After you have exhausted the descriptions of one subject, then choose a new person or thing and a new set of adjectives — and on and on.

Ichabod in *The Tory*. This was the first (of many) off-off-Broadway plays I appeared in after I left the American Academy. I can't identify the actor with the pointed finger, but I appear to be appropriately scolded. This production was directed by Lawrence Sacharow, who later became a noted Obie-winning director and head of the theatre program at Fordham University.

Dr. Hawk in the American (and English language) premiere of *The Portobello Circus*, a Brazilian play translated and directed by producer Jack Brown, at the White Barn Theatre, near Pittsburgh. My legal presentation to Alan Zampese (behind the desk) and his client (unidentified) seems to be working for the moment. I got my Equity card in this season of resident stock (ten plays in ten weeks).

Captain Landry in *Petticoat Fever*, expressing some displeasure at the antics of Curtis Wheeler and Andy Rasbury. This was my second season of resident stock (four plays in eight weeks) at the Duke's Oak Theatre in Cooperstown, New York. Agent Ruth Webb represented me for this job, but I only came to her attention because I invited her to see me in a play in Manhattan (that she didn't attend).

Yellow Feather, attempting to have "my way" with Joan Force in *Little Mary Sunshine*, in my season at the Duke's Oak. The range of roles an actor is given to play in a resident season like this offers an unusual and invaluable training opportunity early in a career, especially for someone who is likely to be cast in "character" roles.

Commodore Roseabove, fleeing for my life, in *Oh Dad, Poor Dad, Someone's Hung You in the Closet and I'm Feelin' So Sad*, in my season of repertory stock (four plays) at the Straight Wharf Theatre, in Nantucket. I might also have been fleeing the clutches of a vicious director (who shall be nameless), whose career turned out to be mercifully short.

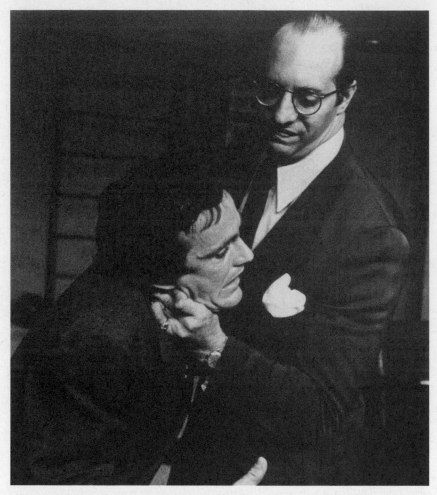

Eddie Fuselli, in a Los Angeles revival of Clifford Odets's *Golden Boy*. A gripping moment in the life of a great theatrical villain. The photo reveals some of the joy I got out of playing this role.

Making my pitch for some space on the front page in *All the President's Men*. This role (as well as my two voice roles as Kenneth Dahlberg and Robert Bennett), in the light of subsequent events, was the most important job of my career. It was my first film with Robert Redford and my first film with the late, great director Alan J. Pakula.

My role as Longly was considerably abbreviated in the final cut of *Close Encounters of the Third Kind*, but director Steven Spielberg generously restored some of my lost moments, including a scene with Academy Award winner Richard Dreyfuss (*The Goodbye Girl*) for the DVD version. Of course, working with a future two-time (so far) Academy Award-winning director was an added bonus.

Having Donald Sutherland as a jogging partner was only one of the joys of working on *Ordinary People*. It was an opportunity for me to work for the third time with Robert Redford and to participate in his first directorial effort, which won Academy Awards for Best Director and Best Picture (among others).

Henry Winkler and I are stunned by the behavior of Michael Keaton (obviously off-camera in this shot), in what was a truly stunning performance in *Night Shift*. Ron Howard, who directed, later won an Academy Award for *A Beautiful Mind*.

In *My Favorite Year*, Peter O'Toole was Academy Award-nominated for this performance. Mark Linn-Baker and I had all we could do to contain (unsuccessfully) his character's outrageous unpredictability in this scene. Director Richard Benjamin, writer Norman Steinberg and a wonderful cast (not to mention producers Michael Gruskoff and Mel Brooks) made this one of the most thoroughly positive experiences of my career.

The Milagro Beanfield War was Robert Redford's second film as director, and our fourth picture together. It was also my second film with M. Emmet Walsh and my second with Academy Award winner Christopher Walken.

When things got really dangerous in *The Double O Kid*, I found good cover behind Hank Garrett's substantial body. Director Duncan McLachlan assembled a terrific group of well-known character actors for this production and I was pleased to be part of it.

Filmed on location in the Soviet Union, this scene from *The Ice Runner* was shot in a Moscow courtroom. A week later, I got a taste of what the Soviet regime was actually like at that time, when the KGB had me locked out of my hotel room (until the production company got my visa extended).

Even in the reverse of this shot in *Pontiac Moon*, Academy Award winner Mary Steen-burgen (*Melvin and Howard*) does her best to hide her face from me while I buy her husband's (played by Ted Danson) eclectic car collection. In typical filmmaking magic, director Peter Medak shot the beginning of this scene and my close-ups in Mendocino, California, and the interior of Mary's house and her close-ups in Pasadena two weeks later.

VI. GETTING THE JOBS ▦

FOR REASONS that escape me, too many so-called professional acting schools and acting teachers treat the employment of actors as an
incidental byproduct of their mission. There are institutions, prestigious universities and so-called conservatories, that proudly proclaim
their "professional school" designation based *only* upon appearances
by a few guest lecturers from the profession who visit the campus
periodically to talk to the students, teaching them very little of value
about doing the homework that gets the jobs. They can do more.

From the very first steps into the profession and throughout the
career, the actor must be able to answer his own question, "What do
I do now?" The school or teacher that doesn't address that fundamental issue is not professional, and for most actors, the "professional"
training they receive under those conditions is less practical than it
needs to be. As a result, the success *rate* for the alumni of those training programs, regardless of the "big names" they advertise, is always
miniscule.

I have been told countless times by many acting school teachers
and administrators that there are not enough jobs to accommodate
the number of actors available and that a high percentage of actors is
bound to fail. It's an attitude guaranteed to produce failed actors. The
fact is that there are hundreds of parts being cast every week in commercials, plays, television and movies — *and there are tens of thousands of actors who won't claim those jobs.* Holding a winning
lottery ticket gets you nothing if you don't show up to claim the
prize. An actor who has done everything he can to get the winning

lottery ticket shouldn't lose the prize because he doesn't know how to claim the award.

The solution is for professional acting schools to offer at least one course on the acting *business*. The focus of that curriculum would be the teaching of salesmanship (locating job opportunities, learning creative common-sense techniques for approaching prospective employers, and public relations). The goal is to get jobs.

When I first began to achieve success in television commercials in New York, Frances Fuller, then president of the American Academy of Dramatic Arts, asked me if I would teach a one-time class in commercials. I declined, but offered instead to teach some professionalism. And so I did. Before the class, one of the students asked me, "Please don't tell us how hard it will be and how many of us will fail." Shocking. It was all they had heard.

I had been less than a marginal professional actor for five years, with fewer than a dozen low-paying jobs and dismal career prospects, before desperation led me into the acting *business*. What that business consisted of was focus, common sense and persistence. In little more than a year, my new, professional approach to acting and the business of acting had produced high-visibility jobs, self-esteem and more income than I had earned in the entire previous five years. A career had begun.

What I taught that class at the American Academy was what I had proven to be true, that fear and inevitability have no place in an actor's career plans. Those students had been inculcated with a time-honored but easily misunderstood axiom that produced many failures but relatively few successes: "Dare to fail." I taught them a new outlook: *"Refuse to fail. Dare to succeed."*

In the years since that first teaching experience, I have introduced some basic, systematic professional concepts to thousands of actors at *all* stages of their careers. I am gratified by the successes achieved by so many who made the effort to beat the odds that had been predicted for them. While there is no attempt here to offer career guidance, I am still obligated to advance a few ideas that are fundamental to a constructive approach to professional acting. The questions and answers in this section will satisfy some of that need and will, I hope, motivate many actors to think about practical aspects of the acting business in a specific and constructive way.

■ *What is "actor's conceit," and why is it important?*

"Actor's conceit" is the expression I use to describe the unfaltering sureness you must have that the role you are playing, preparing to play or auditioning for is yours and only yours and that you have a *right* to it. Just as the playwright or screenwriter copyrights the script, you own the rights to the interpretation and performance of the role. The character's body, voice, mannerisms, gestures, thoughts and, above all, his feelings are your property. *No other actor has a valid claim to that role.*

Without the actor's conceit, your performance (or audition) is doomed. With it, there are no limits to the character's freedom to fully express himself.

■ *What are the two fundamental truths about every script?*

The first thing you must accept as fact about *every* script, before you read even one word, is that it is the best script ever written. Armed with that piece of important irrefutable information, you won't waste valuable time and energy criticizing the material. The expectation of high quality will be the animating force in your work, and you will be inspired to find that quality throughout the script. All your attention will be focused on finding every specific point of excellence. If, for any reason, you are unable to accept the premise of unequalled brilliance, the result for you, the character, the production and the audience will be diminished to the extent of your negativity (unless your lack of confidence in the material so inhibits your performance that you succeed in getting yourself fired). You can only bring out of a script what is in it. You get to decide.

The other fact you must accept about every script you read is that it was written for you. Having that realization will eliminate any possibility that you might, even for a moment, imagine that some other actor could be or should be playing the part. You will be free to explore the infinite possibilities of character, secure in the knowledge that every character choice you make will be correct because the character is uniquely yours.

Knowing that the best script ever written was written for you gives you the freedom (if you accept it) to play the part fearlessly. Even the most experienced actors and the biggest stars are subject to some degree of fear that someone with taste and authority will judge their work to be inadequate. Two-time Academy Award-winning actress Jane Fonda (*Klute* and *Coming Home*) tells a story about her experience working in the picture *Old Gringo*, with Gregory Peck. In watching him deliver a long monologue brilliantly in take after take, she was most affected not by his brilliance but by his fear. She was able to recognize it in him because she sees it in herself. *Every actor is susceptible to fear and self-doubt*. It goes with the territory. Aside from meticulous preparation, the best armament against fear is the security that comes from knowing that you own the role.

Working with the best script ever written also places some responsibility on your shoulders to glorify the material in every way you can and to be most reluctant to change it without having first investigated all the options. From a practical standpoint, every defect you perceive in a script creates an obstacle to your ability to do good work. Give yourself enough obstacles and good work will be impossible.

■ *What is typecasting, and how does it affect an actor's employability?*

Typecasting is the industry's long-standing standard practice of hiring actors according to the essence they project and the kinds of parts they most frequently play. It makes perfect economic sense because, for casting directors, producers and directors, typecasting is as close as they can get to a sure thing.

Actors need to accept the fact of typecasting and to use that knowledge to enhance their own employability. Actors who naturally project obvious castable qualities are fortunate. However, *every* actor can present an equally interesting and compelling presence by attending to one important detail in the work. That detail is character essence.

Most people (actors included) look and behave in ways that categorize them in the most general terms in the minds of most of the people they encounter. But some people project identifiable, interesting qualities more clearly than other people do. Nevertheless, by understanding how most people see him, an actor can reinforce some aspect of those qualities, particularly for his professional photos which precede him into every casting situation.

For auditions, it is vital for an actor to concentrate on the character essence part of the homework so that, even when the actor's personal characteristics do not coincide with the character's requirements, the casting personnel (including director, writers, producers, etc.) get the same indelible, unwavering and appropriate sense of character that they would get from another actor who lived with and exhibited those qualities every day in his personal life.

In *every* instance in which an actor is apparently miscast, the actor has failed to successfully identify and demonstrate an essence of character that believably fulfills the script's demands for that character. It is an acting mistake, not a casting mistake.

■ *How do I approach the part if there are only a few lines of dialogue?*

Every role deserves the same amount of care as any other role, regardless of the number of lines. Your character isn't less of a person just because he only says a few words or because he doesn't appear much in the script. No matter how small the part, your character is the most important character in the script. The script is about your character. Even though your character has only one line (or no lines), his life is as complete as the lives of the characters who appear more prominently in the script.

Don't count the lines. Jane Wyman (*Johnny Belinda*) and Holly Hunter (*The Piano*) both won Academy Awards (for *leading roles*) playing characters who *never* spoke.

There is also a very practical aspect to respecting the complete life of the character. In every scene of every film, the director and the editor need reaction shots of characters observing and listening (and thinking and feeling) as events unfold moment by moment. The characters whose non-speaking moments are the most truthful and interesting will be the ones whose reactions will be used to enhance the tone of the scene and the film.

■ *Is there a special way to approach homework?*

Yes, approach homework with patience and perseverance. There is no limit to the amount of time an actor can spend at home working on his craft or developing a role. There are two tasks, in particular, that the actor is required to complete at home, not at the time and place of his rehearsal or performance. Those two all-important responsibilities are: developing the character and learning the lines.

Homework for the purpose of improving the actor's craft (as opposed to preparing to perform a particular role) is not subject to time limits or completion deadlines. The goal of daily homework is the enhancement of the actor's instrument, not getting through a particular monologue a certain number of times. In fact, an actor who works on his craft most effectively may cover only a few lines (or less) of scripted material in an hour, especially when the truthful source of a particular line of dialogue is difficult to reach.

The process is all about listening to what the character is thinking when he speaks (or when he fails to speak or when he behaves in any other way). Finding that thought (and learning to listen for it) is an all-important part of the character discovery process.

Homework that has a performance goal is a two-part process, and the actor needs to keep the parts separate. The process is the same whether the actor is preparing to audition or to rehearse and perform on the job.

The first part is the exploration. Exploratory acting is the study process that investigates character content and demonstration. It is the step in acting that *always* precedes rehearsal.

The second step in performance-goal homework is the rehearsal process. Rehearsal is reinforcement of exploration's final decisions. *In doing homework for an audition or a job, the actor must be able to finalize the exploration of the material and then begin to rehearse it.* If both parts of this process are not dealt with separately and sufficiently, the work will suffer.

Whether an actor is working on a role for class, for an audition or for his next day on the job, all character work must be done at home. Without the character, there are no words, no movement and no life. Without the *who*, there is no person to audition, to rehearse or to perform. In rehearsal, the actor and the director can only know whether or not the character is valid if there is a character there. In film and television performances, it is unthinkable that an actor's characterization would be different from day to day, from scene to scene.

Finally, learning the lines is such a basic necessity that it is difficult to conceive of an actor not taking that assignment for granted — *and learning the lines means memorizing the lines.* If one actor doesn't know his lines, it is not only his own work that suffers. The work of the director, the work of the other actors and the cost of the entire production are adversely affected.

■ *Isn't the concept of "getting it fast" necessarily superficial, and why is it so difficult for actors to be truthful with only a small amount of preparation?*

"Getting it fast" is only superficial if the actor approaches the role superficially. There are *always* time limits on actors' homework. Cold readings, by their nature, place the greatest time restrictions on the actor, requiring the most systematic, specific, focused approach to the preparation. But, if the actor considers all the issues (Subjective Situation Perception) that affect the character's life and attends to the concepts of character, purpose, feelings and meanings in his audition, the work will be far from superficial.

Actors' work is only untruthful because actors aren't trained to understand the truth and get at it in an uncomplicated, direct way. Time has nothing to do with it. I believe that scene study is the culprit, because it encourages actors to work out character and plot problems in rehearsal instead of at home in concentrated, solitary, personal study. For that reason, stage-trained actors sometimes have difficulty in adapting to the process of getting quick, truthful performances in film, particularly when it comes to repeating unconnected pieces of scenes.

Of course, the cold reading performance isn't as complete as a performance given the luxury of additional discovery and rehearsal time. Nevertheless, it must be complete in the sense of addressing every issue that causes some aspect of the character's feelings and behavior.

■ *How would you characterize the relationship between the actor and the writer?*

The writer is the only creator. The script is the sole authority. It provides a necessary, immovable foundation for the work of all other artistic endeavors involved in the production of a play, television show or motion picture. The original script and all approved rewrites (by the writer or the designated writer, who might be the director or a script doctor) forever remain the authority, and unauthorized changes wrought by an actor, either carelessly or willfully, are destructive to the discovery and truthful communication of the writer's intent.

If the script were to ever cease to be the authority, then the play or television show or film could be anything and about anything, depending only upon what any actor thought (or felt) it might be at any time. In fact, if all the actors got "creative" at the same time, a script with ten characters might be about ten different things with ten different characters on ten different nights of performance or ten different days of shooting. In other words, without the authority of the script, everything that proceeded from it would be a mess.

The actor serves the writer and the script, in total obedience. The actor has a responsibility to listen to *everything* the script tells him about his character, *written and unwritten*. It is vital for the actor to develop his ability to listen to every message (and there is an enormous amount of character information clearly implied in every script, much of it unwritten) supplied by the writer. This also demands that the writer exercise care not to send false messages.

Only one or two words in the narrative or in the dialogue of other characters sometimes offer powerful clues to an actor in his character work, and it is imperative that those clues lead in the direction the writer intends for the character to go.

A few years ago I conducted a workshop called *The Screenwriter and the Actor* for Professor Paul Lucey's graduate screenwriting class at the University of Southern California. I recall one example from that class in which a student's screenplay contained a narrative describing a young boy's startled, speechless reaction to being discovered by his father while he reads one of the father's framed documents on the wall. That one tiny piece of narrative told volumes about the tense relationship between father and son, as well as the son's perception of the father as strict, secretive, menacing, unsettlingly unpredictable or formidable (or maybe all of them). This is invaluable character material for both actors. In the case of that particular screenplay, the writer conveyed what he had intended. If the writer had some other intention or if he had omitted that revealing narrative and the information hadn't been supplied in some other way, both characters' lives would have been adversely affected.

Since the playwright of a new, untried play is usually present during rehearsals, he and the actor have some opportunity to interact, albeit usually through the director. Unfortunately, there is always some unconscious and unnecessary pressure on the actor to please the writer. That pressure tests the actor's ability to concentrate so completely on his acting that there is no room in his head for peripheral concerns.

Screenwriters of feature films (if they are not also the producers or the directors of those films), however, are not usually on the set for all (or any) of the shooting. In the writer's absence, the director makes necessary changes, often in collaboration with the actors. When a scene is added or changed by a skilled and sensitive director, the writer is the beneficiary. I have had the good fortune to be involved in many of those situations, two of which involved Robert Redford and were of great personal benefit to me.

The first was the film *All the President's Men*, directed by Alan J. Pakula, starring Robert Redford and produced by his company, Wildwood Enterprises. Alan felt that one of the scripted *Washington Post* budget meeting scenes lacked a certain reality that would be enhanced by the participation of some of the less important characters.

My contribution was an improvised moment based on a contemporaneous news item from that newspaper. It was easy to imagine my assistant editor character's enthusiasm and boldness in pitching my story for space on the front page (which I got). Then we rehearsed it and shot it.

That scene, as small as it was in the context of the entire film, gave me a few significant moments on screen with some wonderful actors including Jack Warden, Academy Award winner Martin Balsam (*A Thousand Clowns*), and Jason Robards, whose performance would win him his first Academy Award (his second was for *Julia*). Screenwriter William Goldman won his second Academy Award for his screenplay (his first was for *Butch Cassidy and the Sundance Kid*).

Several years later Robert Redford directed his first picture, *Ordinary People*, which includes a party scene with many actors, some of whom he asked to improvise conversation. The improvised dialogue that Bob liked was rehearsed and shot. Again, my new moments (which I based on the supercilious cocksureness of my character that Alvin Sargent had already created and scripted in another scene) were included, and, again, I benefited from an enhanced presence in an acclaimed film. *Ordinary People* went on to win several Academy Awards including, among others, Best Picture, Best Director for Robert Redford and Best Supporting Actor for Timothy Hutton. Alvin Sargent won his second Academy Award for his screenplay (his first was for *Julia*).

Without the structure and tone supplied by the writer, producing a coherent play or film would be nearly impossible. For that reason alone, every actor (and director) needs to apply himself to the task of finding and serving the writer's intentions.

Sometimes, however, the script, itself (because of errors or inconsistencies of grammar, logic, historical fact, etc.), defeats the writer's objectives. When those occurrences are discovered by the actor, *and it is the actor's job to discover them quickly*, he *must* call them to the attention of the production person to whom he is closest or with whom he feels that he can most comfortably (and tactfully) broach the subject.

■ *What are "Cornerstones of Truth"?*

There are four *essential* ingredients in every performance (and every audition). They are necessary because every moment of a character's existence contains them, all four of them. These ingredients are so important that I call them "Cornerstones of Truth." They are cornerstones because without any one of them the performance collapses. The four cornerstones are: character, purpose, feelings and meanings.

The first cornerstone, character, refers specifically to essence of character. The essence of a person is the most important determinant of his feelings and behavior at all times. Without character, there would be no person in the scene.

The second cornerstone, purpose, provides the reason for the character's participation in the scene. The character always has a reason (and a need) to be there. Except in rare cases, the reasons are the character's reasons, not the reasons of other characters (be aware of other characters' attempts to deter you from your purpose, as well as your character's desires to deter them from theirs; the conflicts that result from these cross purposes produce important manifestations of character). Without the character's purpose, the actor could go home — and the audience *will* go home.

The third cornerstone, feelings, how the character feels at all times, is a necessity because without them the character would be lifeless.

The fourth cornerstone, meanings, refers to the character's intention in every word he speaks, every choice not to speak and every movement and gesture. Obviously, this requires careful attention to *all* the details of speech and action.

Truthful clarity is the actor's first and most basic requirement in every performance (and every audition). Characters *need* to be truthful (to who they are) in everything they say and do, and actors need to be sure that every truthful moment is fulfilled *and communicated*. If every moment is truthful and that moment is communicated clearly, then the actor will have achieved truthful clarity. As a result, each moment will also be original and interesting.

For the great television writer William Blinn (*Roots*, *Brian's Song* and many others), the writer's responsibility to the truth is a requirement, but it is not his only requirement. In the first two productions of his play, *Walking Peoria*, I had the good fortune to play a character (a writer named Raymond Poole) whose ideas about the television business are profound, and he expresses them eloquently. At one point in this excellent play, there is no doubt that Poole is speaking for William Blinn when he says that the writer's responsibility is to "just tell the truth in an interesting way." *That is also the actor's responsibility, and nothing less will suffice.*

■ *How will I know if I should use an accent or dialect?*

The character will inform you about all aspects of his speech. Be faithful to the geography of the character's life, as well as his education, his station in life and his essence. Ideally, the character's accent (foreign or American regional) or dialect (which usually means American regional) should be perfectly representative of what the actor's research indicates it to be. If the actor cannot effectively produce the accent, then he needs to get a speech coach. Don't compromise on this point.

If you have a distinct regionalism in your everyday speech and if your character is identified as someone for whom that regionalism would make no sense, then some accommodation has to be made. Either you allow the character to speak as the script indicates he would, or the script must be altered to make the character speak as you do (the autobiographical acting concept). Of course, the inconsistency could be allowed to stand, in which case the actor winds up looking a little silly.

In *The Ultimate Warrior*, the character played by Yul Brynner (Academy Award winner in *The King and I*) identifies himself to Max Von Sydow's character in these memorable words, "My name eez Car-r-rson. I'm fr-r-rom Detr-r-roit." It would have made no difference to the story if the name of the character and his native city had been changed to coincide with Yul Brynner's accent (which never changed throughout his career). But the change wasn't made, and the unintended result was giggling and snickering from the audience.

There have been other notable occasions in which the actor's inflexible star presence seemed to overshadow logic. The excellent British character actor Claude Rains, a major star from the 1930s to the 1960s playing a wide variety of roles, many of them seemingly indistinguishable one from another, played the French Captain Louis Renault in *Casablanca* to great acclaim (which included receiving one of his four Academy Award nominations) without attempting to use a French accent. Likewise, two-time Academy Award winner Spencer Tracy (*Captains Courageous* and *Boys Town*) never distanced himself very far from some of his own apparent personal traits, even to playing the very British *Dr. Jekyll and Mr. Hyde* with his own American dialect.

Great star power rarely overcomes the audience's desire for the actor's work to make some sense. And when a star (or any other actor) adds an appropriate and effective dialect or accent to the characterization, as in the work of Academy Award winners Kevin Kline (*A Fish Called Wanda*) in *French Kiss*, Renee Zellweger (*Cold Mountain*) in *Bridget Jones's Diary*, Robert Duvall (*Tender Mercies*) in *A Shot at Glory*, Sir Ben Kingsley (*Ghandi*) in *House of Sand and Fog*, Anthony Quinn (*Viva Zapata* and *Lust for Life*) in *Zorba the Greek*, and Meryl Streep's Academy Award-winning performance in *Sophie's Choice*, the audience is better able to forget that the actor is even there.

Generally speaking, an actor shouldn't use an accent to accommodate the original language of a script that has been translated into English. For example, playing Oedipus with a Greek accent or Doctor Zhivago with a Russian accent would be silly. It would be equally ludicrous to do a production of *Romeo and Juliet* in which all the characters speak in Italian accents just because the setting is Italy and all the characters are Italian.

Sometimes producers make casting choices in order to achieve status or box office appeal for the production without regard for the actors' glaring inappropriate speech differences. In *Holocaust*, a star-studded television miniseries, the accents ranged from German to British to general American to Brooklyn, even among characters born in the same country, raised in the same neighborhoods and even within a single family. Perhaps such inconsistencies are not thought to make much of a difference to the financial success of the producers. I wonder how that can be true, because they *always* make a difference to the audience.

VII. DOING THE JOB

FOR MOST ACTORS, the *quest* for employment seems to be a career of its own. That illusion is a good thing if it keeps the actor meaningfully and purposefully occupied in pursuit of his goal. But it isn't his real work. Once the actor is hired, the real stuff begins, and it begins from the moment the actor is officially employed.

A thoroughly professional actor approaches every detail of acting with diligence. That includes not only the concentration on homework to achieve completeness of character and deliver a good performance every time, but also adherence to consistently high standards of professionalism in *every other aspect of the work, which will lead to greater character development and a better performance.*

What I have concentrated on in this section are some of the less obvious but very important aspects of the actor's work. Attention to these elements can not only enhance the performance, but also gain the appreciation, cooperation and maybe even the admiration of other professionals involved in the production.

■ *How important is the actor's attitude in the workplace, and can you explain what constitutes a positive attitude on the job?*

I believe that the actor's attitude (and corresponding behavior) at work is so important that its importance can't be overestimated.

A positive attitude could be defined as a spirit of harmony and cooperation. It also demonstrates a high level of professionalism. One person's attitude can have such an effect, positive or negative, on *everyone* in the vicinity, that the level of everyone else's work is elevated or diminished. Furthermore, the actor, by his attitude, creates an indelible emotional memory in the minds of those he works with. That memory can make a difference, apart from acting considerations, when the time comes for the director to cast a future project.

On a personal note, I am certain that some producers and directors have hired me more than once because I brought some degree of harmony (in addition to the acting) to work with me. On the other hand, it is also possible that some momentary, seemingly insignificant flash of temper or non-cooperation, long forgotten, provided enough of a subconscious (or conscious) reason for me not to be rehired by some directors. I will never know. The unknowable effect of small intangibles should be enough to keep most smart actors behaving themselves. I recommend that actors practice exemplary behavior for its own sake.

I have been blessed to not only witness, but to be the recipient of countless examples of professional courtesies extended to me by actors whose stardom might have given them license to behave differently. I will recount some of those instances here. It is important to note that in each case, if the actor had not gone out of his way for me, no one would have noticed.

Stars want the workplace to be harmonious, and they are often the most visible instigators of that mood. *At Long Last Love*, directed by Peter Bogdanovich, was my first movie in Hollywood. Burt Reynolds, who stars in that film, perfectly demonstrated an attitude of harmony from the moment he walked onto the set. It made no difference to Burt that I was an unknown actor playing the smallest role in the picture. He walked up to me, stuck out his hand and said, "Hi, I'm Burt Reynolds." I should recall that moment more often. It would make me a better person.

The first television miniseries I ever appeared in was *The Money-changers* in the role of Stanley Inchbeck. One of my scenes was a telephone conversation with the character played by the distinguished Christopher Plummer, and it was our only scene together. Even though he wasn't scheduled to work until several hours later, Chris came down to the set to read his *off-camera* lines with me. A year later the same courtesy was extended to me in my second episode of *M*A*S*H* by Harry Morgan, who played Colonel Potter.

Working late at night on location for an episode of *Columbo*, we stopped shooting for a dinner break. Peter Falk had finished his work for the day, except that we still had to shoot my close-ups in one of our scenes. Peter sent one of the assistant directors to me to ask if I wanted Peter to stay for his off-camera lines. I declined because it wasn't critical to my performance, and Peter had already put in a very long day. *But he was willing to stay as a courtesy to me.* Peter Falk habitually goes out of his way for other actors, even to reshoot scenes to accommodate other actors' needs.

For the jogging scene in *Ordinary People*, Donald Sutherland and I had been running for several hours when the time came to shoot my close-up. It would have been no problem to get a tall stunt man to run with me for the eye lines, since I had all the dialogue. But that option wouldn't even have occurred to Donald Sutherland. So Donald ran with me for my close-up for the sole purpose of making *my* performance better.

Harmonious sets are the norm, not the exception, in the film business. And that tone is always set by the director, the producer and the stars. It is incumbent upon everyone working on a film to contribute to the director's mission, not only by doing his own work, but by being gracious and appreciative of everybody else's contribution. I have seen this in operation time after time after time, and I have endeavored to do my part. It is one of the many rewarding aspects of the acting business.

■ *Will I always be given a complete script?*

You will not always be given a complete script. But you must always ask. If it's a play, and it's been published or previously produced, then the script exists and you should have it. The motion picture and television industry standard is for the producer to deliver the complete script (with up-to-date revisions) to the actor on the day the actor is hired and to continue to deliver daily changes until the actor has completed his work. In some rare circumstances, you will not get a complete script or even get to read the complete script. This happens for a variety of reasons, sometimes known only to the director, and when it does you just have to deal with it. You must never assume that the audition script will be the shooting script. They are rarely the same.

In television, especially dramatic episodic television, incomplete scripts are extremely rare. But in the half-hour comedy format, massive changes are made constantly, sometimes right up to the last pickup shot on the last day of shooting or the final taping. When I did *Barney Miller*, the regular cast alerted me to expect late nights to accommodate last minute rewrites, and the predictions proved to be correct. Because we knew the routine, the actors were able to pace ourselves, but the writer, Reinhold Weege, with whom I later worked when he produced *Night Court* and *Park Place*, was always under the gun and the clock, creating wonderfully funny stuff at all hours, and he looked like he had been through Hell.

Except for the stars of the film, none of the actors in *Close Encounters of the Third Kind* ever got to see the entire screenplay. Steven Spielberg, who wrote the script and directed (and later won Academy Awards for directing *Schindler's List* and *Saving Private Ryan*), was very protective of the uniqueness of his story. Consequently, very few actors got to see more than their own scenes. Virtually trapped on location in Mobile, Alabama, I asked Steven if I could just borrow the script to read it. He declined.

Other directors, including Woody Allen and three-time Academy Award nominee Richard Brooks, are reputed to have withheld certain completed screenplays from the actors. It is said that Brooks sometimes gave out current scene pages at the beginning of each day and collected them before the actors left the set. When a director has an innovative idea and the project has taken years to develop at a cost of many millions of dollars, the paranoia is understandable and justified.

There may also be times when you will begin shooting a film before the screenplay is finished. When I started work on *The Electric Horseman*, the script was incomplete and was still unfinished when I left the picture. Several months later, Robert Redford, Jane Fonda, John Saxon, James Sikking, Nicolas Coster and I returned to Utah for our final scenes. As unnerving as it may be at times, unpredictability also provides an additional element of excitement to this business.

■ *What do you mean when you say, "Break down the script to energize it"?*

Scripts are literary devices. The literary form (in which all scripts are written) produces nothing living except what comes to life in the reader's imagination. All literary characters are imaginary, *until the actor demonstrates the living, breathing, behaving humanity.* For me, an actor's only job is to reveal and play the character. To accomplish that end, I urge actors to refer to Subjective Situation Perception as a reliable guide and basis for that discovery. The logic of that outline will lead to every aspect of the character's life, including purpose, feelings, relationship conflicts and obstacles that naturally occur within every scene, even when the character is silent.

Discovery of character, however, isn't enough. The character needs to *demonstrate* in behavior what has been revealed to the actor in the discovery process. In order to demonstrate character, the actor has to *energize* the material by breaking down the script into beats (this is most easily accomplished by placing a vertical pencil line between lines of dialogue where beat changes occur; it is also necessary to note in the script where those changes occur when there is no dialogue). The energizing elements in each beat are *feelings* and *tempo*. Without those two elements, the performance is nothing but a report. With them, the character freely expresses himself, and he will do that, moment by moment, *energizing the written material into living reality.* Obedience to the character's emotions and the tempo or pulse with which he expresses them will insulate the actor from indicated acting decisions. The character's *real* behavior is the goal.

■ *Should I approach every script in the same way, and are there guidelines I can follow?*

When you work on a script, there are some things you must do because they are so basic and so logical. In the sense that you will include each of these fundamental steps to some degree, you will be approaching every script in the same way. The process should be much the same whether it is a play, a teleplay or a screenplay. Here are some suggestions and a reasonable order to follow:

1. Read the entire script very carefully to absorb as much information as you possibly can. Take as much time (and as many readings) as you need to learn the story, but form no opinions and do no character analysis. These readings are for information only and are extremely important because, as the actor, you need to know and absorb everything in the script that has even the remotest connection to your character (even though the character himself may know nothing about some of the details).

2. Read the script as the character to begin to personalize (*feel*) every piece of information that affects your (the character's)

life. This reading will give you a sense of the continuity of the character's progression through the story. Repeat this step as many times as necessary, and use this step to begin memorizing the lines. Learning the lines thoroughly and quickly is fundamental to doing good work.

3. Read the script (referring to the Subjective Situation Perception outline) to fully explore the details of the character's life. Find and describe the character's essence. Allow feelings and behavior to develop. Repeat any portion of this step as many times as necessary.

4. Say the character's lines from the essence of the character, relating particularly to relationships with other characters. Repeat any portion of this step as many times as necessary.

5. Solidify your memorization, continuing to develop the character's essence, feelings and behavior.

6. Break down the script to energize it.

7. Locate every instance of possible physical touching of other characters. Rehearse those moments using a physical object (or person) to represent the character to be touched so that you (the *actor*) aren't awkward or self-conscious in performing the action.

8. Find references to every prop (including furniture, set and non-human living creatures) that the character touches in every scene. Include props that are necessary and appropriate to the character, even if they aren't mentioned in the script. Work the props into the dialogue until the words and the action become natural to the character (letting the character finalize his own level of expertise).

9. Find wardrobe references in every scene, paying particular attention to items of apparel that the character puts on or takes

off during the scene. Those incidents must be rehearsed with the dialogue until they become natural (to the character, in character).

10. Continue to rehearse, exploring all aspects of the character's environment and the feelings and behavior that are generated.

Note: In every instance above in which I use the word "rehearse," I mean for the task to be done as homework, not on the time and at the expense of the rest of the company.

There is no one best way to approach a script that will suit the needs and the temperament of every actor. Furthermore, every acting situation presents unique conditions (time constraints, script changes, etc.), so that actors cannot become inflexibly wedded to a single way of working. Each actor has to discover his own way (and a somewhat different way every time) through the uncertain, painstaking and sometimes painful territory of character exploration, rehearsal and, ultimately, performance.

The suggestions I make are for the purpose of offering the actor some practical aid through the process, not to remake every actor's way of working to agree with mine. Many actors will find the suggestions helpful.

■ *Do I need to memorize the part, word for word?*

Yes. The most important reason for memorizing word for word is to respect the character's way of expressing himself. The scripted dialogue is the only authority for this most important character source material, and if the words are changed, it is likely that some other element of the character is also changed. The character's speech may be an indicator of his intellectual, educational, mental, emotional, spiritual, cultural or physical components, and maybe others as well. Allow the character to reveal himself through his own words instead of imposing your decisions on him.

Another reason for being careful about the words is that the writer and the director might be really happy with the script as it was written. Don't assume that, after the years they spent developing the script, they will be pleased to hear whatever you come up with (some directors will request dialogue creation from the actor *after* they see what he does with the material he has been given; it would be wise to wait for that invitation).

The second film I did after I arrived in Hollywood was *Lucky Lady*, starring Burt Reynolds and Academy Award winners Gene Hackman (*The French Connection* and *Unforgiven*) and Liza Minnelli (*Cabaret*), and directed by the great Stanley Donen (who, since then, has been honored with an Academy Award for his brilliant career). In shooting my only scene in the film (a scene which included the three stars), one of the supporting actors (not I, fortunately) repeated one of his words twice, apparently to achieve some degree of emphasis. Stanley stopped the take to ask the actor how many times the word appeared in that sentence. The actor replied, "Once." Stanley's response was very short, to the point and quite humorless. "Then let's just hear it once. Otherwise, we'll have a very long scene and a very boring movie." Being embarrassed on a set isn't fun. Spare yourself.

In addition to the need to memorize the lines, however, actors also have to be adaptable to momentary script changes from writers and directors. Playwrights always attend rehearsals of their new plays because the contributive, collaborative efforts of directors and actors inform writers about the actual performability of what they have written. Consequently, extensive rewrites from the playwright are common during the theatrical rehearsal process.

Feature film scripts also change during production, and actors always have to be prepared to adapt to last minute, sometimes substantial dialogue changes. Those changes might be necessitated by anything from a major traffic detour at a location to a previous script change that doesn't make sense without clarification.

I remember riding in the car in St. George, Utah, from the hotel to the *The Electric Horseman* set when the director Sydney Pollack casually handed me new pages of script, saying "Here's your new speech." The good news for actors in big budget movies is that the pace of shooting (two or three script pages per day) allows extra time to learn new material. In episodic television and in films with smaller budgets, the new stuff has to be absorbed more quickly.

Regardless of the amount of time the actor has available to memorize the lines and integrate his actions with those lines, he has to accomplish it with certainty and thoroughness. In theatre, actors almost always have some rehearsal time to work new material into the performance (except in cases of tryouts of new plays in which the playwright might put in new lines at *any* time). And when an actor makes a mistake during a performance on stage, there's no one to say "Cut, let's take it again." He gets through it one way or another and the moment passes.

In television and films, even though almost any moment can be reshot (under most circumstances), there is still, nevertheless, very little room for actors' mistakes (momentary lapses notwithstanding). Every retake costs money, and the more complicated the scene and the more stars in the scene, the more costly the retakes. When I worked with director Blake Edwards (an Academy Award honoree for his extraordinary body of work as a director, writer and producer) in *Switch*, we shot several entire, long, complicated scenes without cuts (and no coverage), and in those instances every mistake by an actor (or anyone else) necessitated time-consuming resets by props, wardrobe, makeup, lights, camera, etc., sometimes nullifying good work by the other actors.

Even when everything goes smoothly, some scenes can take many hours to shoot, so the actor has to be at the top of his game at all times.

Memorizing lines is the easiest part of the actor's game. The words have to be so thoroughly committed to memory that they can be repeated flawlessly under any and all circumstances of production and regardless of the actor's own personal physical, mental, or emotional condition on that particular day. In *Down with Love*, there is a long boardroom scene in which Renee Zellweger's character has most of the dialogue and speaks all of it quickly and smartly, including one rapid-fire monologue. We shot that scene for two days. Renee was a wonder to behold. Her energy never lagged, her concentration never faltered, she never dropped a single word, *not even once* and her performance was on the money on every take. That high standard of excellence in all aspects of her work paid off for Renee with her Academy Award- winning performance in *Cold Mountain* the following year. It is not uncommon for star actors to be that focused in the work. That is how they got there. Memorizing the lines, as absolutely necessary as it is, is only a small part of it.

A word of caution: Even though the words are sacred, the punctuation isn't. Scripts are written in literary form, with commas, periods, etc., appearing in grammatically correct places. Natural spoken language follows no such rules. Don't allow the writer's punctuation to inhibit the character's impulses in phrasing his speech as his thoughts and feelings of the moment dictate.

■ *When is it appropriate to ask questions about the work, and how do I know whom to ask?*

It is appropriate to ask questions *every* time you are unsure about some necessity of the work, *if asking is the only way to get the answer*. Be thorough in your own preparation, so that you aren't asking someone else to do your work for you.

In an audition situation, if you have questions that need to be answered because the answers will affect your reading in a positive way, ask them before you read. Ideally, you will have had the foresight to ask the casting department (either directly or through your representative) before you complete your homework. If that isn't possible, try to get the answer from a casting assistant or receptionist before you get into the audition room. Failing in that, the person to ask is the person who speaks to you immediately before the actual reading begins. Never ask questions that have nothing to do with the material before you read; and never leave vital questions about the material unasked.

After you have been hired, important character questions should be addressed to the director, but only if your own diligent homework can't provide the answer. Questions (and character suggestions) about makeup, props and wardrobe should be directed to the professionals in charge of those departments in the production.

When shooting on film or tape, you must always understand the technical requirements of the shot as it applies to you. You have to be sure of the eye lines, the size of the frame and the precise point in the script that will begin the shot. The script supervisor and the camera operator are excellent sources of that information. Asking is easy, and your simple request for the information will demonstrate an aspect of your professionalism, as well as saving the producers some time and money.

■ *In film and television, does an actor have to give the same performance and his best performance in every take?*

Yes, although the "same" doesn't necessarily mean identical in every respect. When I say that the performances must be the same, I mean the same interpretation and the same intensity. When filming begins, the experimentation is over, *unless the director wants it to be different.*

There are good reasons why the actor's work has to be consistent from take to take, not the least of which is courtesy to the other actors, whose performances may be adversely affected when one person's spontaneous inspiration alters the meaning of the moment or the scene. Every actor has the right to expect that his close-up will receive the same intensity from every other actor's performance off-camera as that actor gave in his own close-up.

Another reason for maintaining uniformity is that by the time the director is ready to shoot the scene, he is satisfied with what he saw in the final rehearsal and expects to see the same thing in the first take. He expects every take to be the actor's best. Furthermore, the director, the cinematographer and the sound mixer have set the timing of the scene, and sometimes even the smallest variations can necessitate retakes which cost time and money. If an actor's work in one take doesn't match (is inconsistent because of performance, eye line, wardrobe or for any other reason) with other takes of the same scene, that actor's carelessness might cause the director to use another actor's close-up of the same moment, thereby costing the offending actor valuable screen time.

Perhaps the best reason for the actor to sustain a high level of performance through all the takes is that he never knows which take will be in the film. In *My Favorite Year*, we had a scene in which Benjy Stone, played by Mark Linn-Baker, brings in a bag of breakfast pastries and coffee for himself and the other writers, Sy Benson, Alice Miller and Herb Lee, played, respectively, by Bill Macy, Anne DeSalvo and me. Sy impulsively reaches for his coffee, grabs a container, rips the top off, takes a swig and spits it back into the cup. Benjy says, "That's Herb's tea." Then Sy hands me the cup of tea and saliva, and I stare at it.

We shot the master, and Richard Benjamin, who directed the picture wonderfully, said, "Print." Then I got what I must have thought was a brilliant idea (and I now have no idea what it might have been). Assuming that we would, of course, reshoot the scene (another master shot, two-shots, close-ups, etc.), I enthusiastically said to Richard, "Are we going to reshoot this?" His response was quick and typically funny (Richard Benjamin's sense of humor, among other qualities, makes him a joy to work with.). "You mean in our lifetime? No."

Everything Richard wanted from that scene was in the one and only master shot. If even one of the actors had saved his best performance for his close-up, all of us would have just been out of luck.

■ *Will the director direct me?*

Possibly, but maybe not in the way you need, want or expect. Every director wants the acting to be as good as it can be, but they all have different standards and they each have their own methods for reaching that goal.

What drives many actors crazy is the director who doesn't direct them, doesn't seem to pay particular attention to them or doesn't constantly compliment and reassure them. The director's inattention probably means that the director approves of what the actor is doing. It might even mean that he loves it. The *seemingly* inattentive director usually doesn't comment on work that he likes because he is too occupied with matters that *require* his attention. Some directors just don't do a lot of complimenting, and that is something actors have to get used to (one of the reasons why actors need to find their security in their own work and not rely on the approval of others to validate their contribution).

Sometimes actors should count their blessings when directors ignore them. There are certain directors who have been known to verbally brutalize and humiliate actors whose work doesn't satisfy them. In an interview in *The Los Angeles Times* many years ago, Academy Award- winning actor George C. Scott (*The Hustler*, *Patton*) commented on actors' vulnerability by saying, "Having a director like Otto Preminger jumping up and down on the set screaming, 'You have no talent!' doesn't help." Fortunately, that kind of behavior by directors is extremely rare.

Some of the best directors I have worked with were able to get optimum performances out of actors with minimal directorial suggestion. Alan J. Pakula, a great actor's director who I worked with twice (*All the President's Men* and *Comes a Horseman*) used the phrase, "What if…," meaning, what if your character did something differently, or did this thing instead of that thing. Alan wanted to see everything the actor came up with on his own, and more.

Academy Award-winning director Sydney Pollack (*Out of Africa*), an actor and a former acting teacher, is also a great actor's director. When we did *The Electric Horseman*, I noted that Sydney approaches actors gently, seemingly with deference, even in matters of blocking, which he frequently lets the actors find first, with questions (instead of autocratic direction) like, "Can you do the same thing seated?" Like every other good director I've worked with, he encourages the actor's creativity. One day on the set during a break in the shooting, I noticed Sydney writing furiously and asked him what he was work-ing on. "The next scene, and I expect contributions," was the response. And he has a very keen sense of what works and what doesn't (what is truthful and what isn't). Sydney is one of the most perceptive and uncompromising acting performance directors in the business, which is one of the reasons so many good actors trust him and want to work with him (Robert Redford, another great Academy Award-winning actor's director, has worked as an actor with Sydney *seven* times). When Academy Award winner Dustin Hoffman (*Kramer vs. Kramer* and *Rain Man*) did *Tootsie* for Sydney, they apparently had a few disagreements along the way. Sydney tells it like this: "We'd go into my trailer and argue about it for half an hour. Then we'd come out and do it my way — most of the time." I'm sure Sydney's "way" contributed to Dustin's well-deserved Academy Award nomination for that performance.

Three-time Academy Award-winning director William Wyler (*Mrs. Miniver*, *The Best Years of our Lives* and *Ben-Hur*) was a noted perfectionist, for which he and his actors paid the price. At the end of a long and distinguished career, Wyler was being honored by the American Film Institute. In working with editor John Simpson (who later directed me in a production of Lanford Wilson's *Serenading Louie*) to compile clips from his films, Wyler watched a scene he wanted to use from *Wuthering Heights*. John heard Wyler moan, "The scene needs a close-up." In his mind Wyler was still trying to reshoot his classic film *forty years later*.

Charlton Heston once remarked on the workout Wyler put his actors through, then finished with, "But you come out smelling like a rose." Indeed. Heston won the Best Actor Academy Award for his performance as Ben-Hur. William Wyler only demanded from his actors what he knew they could give. When asked how he always got such good performances from his actors, Wyler responded, "I always hired good actors."

Billy Wilder, Academy Award-winning director of *The Lost Weekend* and *The Apartment*, was also famous for painstaking patience when he wasn't getting what he wanted from an actor. Two-time Academy Award-winning actor Jack Lemmon (*Mr. Roberts* and *Save the Tiger*), who worked with Wilder many times, tells about one of his first experiences with the director. On one particular shot Wilder kept saying "Let's shoot it again. Do less, Jack." After many takes, the exasperated Lemmon said, "Billy, if I do any less, I won't be acting at all." To which Wilder replied, "Now you got it, Jack."

There is no predictability in directors. But directors all have one thing in common. Every director does his best to get the performances that work for his production. Directors can't be expected to teach acting or do the acting — and they won't. That is what they hire the actors for. It is always up to the actor to bring his best stuff to the stage or the set. Directors like to be surprised with qualities of character that they didn't see in the material and haven't expected.

■ *Will the director direct me before I begin to act?*

I hope not. Most directors won't direct an actor until they see what the actor's homework and instincts have produced. For a director to direct an actor before the actor has shown his work would be like the policeman who directs traffic before the cars arrive.

A few years ago, I was working on a film with an interesting (unusual) and funny character actor named George Furth (also the author of the Broadway musical, *Company*). George and I were on the set for our first day's work. Before we started to rehearse, the director (whose name I won't mention) began to describe in detail every nuance of the scene and how he wanted us to play it. Every nuance. As I listened to the director's short, well-meaning but ill-conceived speech, I glanced at George, whose face had become quite red, and it seemed as though a vein in his neck had begun to throb. Then, without warning, George blurted out, "*Dontyouwanttoseewhatwedobeforeyoudirectus?*" ("Don't you want to see what we do before you direct us?") The moment was startling, but very effective. We weren't pre-directed again (the director has never directed another film).

Directors sometimes offer what they believe to be helpful (but not vital) suggestions to actors before they audition for roles. My own instinct is to reject, as gently as possible, "helpful" pre-audition direction.

Just before I began my reading for the role of Drollhauser, the attorney in *Night Shift*, the excellent director Ron Howard (who later won an Academy Award for *A Beautiful Mind*) offered to give me his concept of the character. I respectfully declined because I was confident with my own preparation, and I didn't want to discard it out of an obligation to give him a split-second rendition of his version. Besides, he would have had the option of directing me after seeing what I came up with. It was also important to me that Ron see the kind of work that I would bring to the set if he hired me to play the part (which he did).

Some actors want to hear everything a director has to say even before they read, and that approach might actually work for many of them. I have my doubts. Trying to correctly and instantly interpret and demonstrate the words of a director (especially a famous director) in the midst of pre-audition pressure is more likely to dismantle the character you have developed and embodied than it is to enhance the character. It is possible that the exact thing he wanted was what you had prepared, but, unfortunately, you misinterpreted his explanation. Most directors, particularly the good ones, want the original magic that comes out of you. The actor's most powerful creative tools are his instincts, and no good director wants to take those away from him.

An actor is hired for his uniqueness and his originality, in addition to his appropriateness for the role he has been hired to play. The director wants to see what that originality produces before he imposes his own ideas on it.

Directors are usually very happy with actors' choices. In my experience, most directors *want* to be happy with actors' choices, and they *expect* to be happy with those choices.

■ *What does a director mean when he says, "Make it bigger"?*

Actors need to be very cautious about taking the direction "Make it bigger" at face value. If some elements of character are unclear or obscure, the director might just be requesting more detail or more clarity, in which case the character can reveal additional truthful aspects of his behavior. But if the director means that he just wants more demonstrative "stuff" because the camera shot requires it or for some other reason that is divorced from the truth of the character or his situation, then the actor needs to protect himself (and the character) by requesting a more understandable and more usable direction.

There have been two significant instances in my own career in which I was directed to make it bigger, and the results were very different. It happened both times on major studio films.

In a picture directed by Peter Medak (who directed the memorable

Let Him Have It and *The Ruling Class*, among others), my character had a nervous condition and a speech impediment which were quite obvious to anyone who was near him. But because the character was first revealed in a long shot, Peter wanted the character's afflictions bigger. So I made them bigger. On film, the excessive symptoms merely appeared to be caricaturish and false. The scene was unusable, and my character was cut from the film.

Perhaps, if I had been more subservient to the character, even the "bigger" behavior would have been believable. But it wasn't to be and, even though we never discussed it, Peter apparently forgave me for my destruction of that character. I've had the good fortune to work three times with him after that, including the classic three-character *Twilight Zone* episode, "Button, Button," with Mare Winningham and Brad Davis.

The other instance in which I was directed to make it bigger was during the filming of the aforementioned *My Favorite Year*, produced by Mel Brooks and Michael Gruskoff, for whom I had previously worked in *Lucky Lady*, and written by Norman Steinberg, who had written *Blazing Saddles* for Mel. I was playing a television writer named Herb Lee (a thinly disguised Neil Simon), a character who went through the entire film inaudibly whispering all of his dialogue (except for one short exclamation). The director, Richard Benjamin, gave me a general note telling me that it could be bigger. Inaudible but bigger, meaning Herb's non-verbal behavior. I felt uneasy about complying, because my instincts told me that the behavior I had found in Herb was big enough. Richard said, "Trust me." So I did. I discovered that if I allowed Herb to really enjoy the power he derived from not speaking, he would become truthfully more demonstrative of his feelings, and it worked. More subtle behavior from Herb wouldn't have been as effective. Richard was absolutely right.

The "make it bigger" direction is unusual, particularly in film, because the camera records very small details. On stage, the actor might hear it more often, but even then, *the character* has to do it.

The actor must always know *exactly* what the director means and be able to translate it into character terms.

■ *What does a director mean when he says, "Bring it down" or "It's over the top"?*

When directors use expressions like "It's too big," "Bring it down" or "It's over the top," they almost always mean that what the actor is doing is not truthful. *Size has nothing to do with it.* Truthfulness that comes out of character and circumstance, unless the character is inappropriate to the material (which *always* means that the actor imposed himself on the material), is never too big. The long and brilliant careers of Peter O'Toole, Kirk Douglas and Academy Award winners Bette Davis (*Dangerous* and *Jezebel*), Jack Nicholson (*One Flew Over the Cuckoo's Nest*, *Terms of Endearment* and *As Good As It Gets*), George C. Scott and Al Pacino offer numerous vivid examples of truthful acting unrestrained by considerations of bigness.

In my own experience, insecurity, fear or false fearlessness sometimes misled me into overdone acting choices, especially early in my career. Fortunately for me, kind, caring and very influential people were often around to save me from myself. Just such an instance occurred during the shooting of my first movie, *Lady Liberty*, directed by the great Italian director Mario Monicelli (*Big Deal on Madonna Street*, *The Organizer*, three Italian Foreign Language Academy Award selections, etc.).

A long evening of filming and the imminent moment of my close-ups in a scene with the beautiful star of the film, Academy Award winner Sophia Loren (*Two Women*), must have sent my energy level "over the top." The crew had just about finished setting up the lights when I noticed Sophia, sitting a few feet away, looking at me. I smiled. Then she smiled and said, softly and sweetly, "Do less." It was a great acting note because it so succinctly brought my performance back to reality.

If you are ever asked to make your performance smaller, your first attention should be to the truthfulness of the work. There are no size limitations on truthful acting. If the work is truthful, very few directors would ever try to "correct" it. And if you are faking it (indicating), then no amount of size reduction will be able to miraculously transform it into truthfulness. You can't improve a big, empty performance by making it smaller. You will only wind up with a tiny, empty performance.

■ *If I'm directed to do the scene faster or slower or bigger or smaller or louder or quieter, how can I make that quick adjustment without being artificial?*

Production pressures may cause even a very good director to be less communicative than he might be in a calmer moment (or less communicative than the actor thinks he should be). Some directors always speak in shorthand. But regardless of how result-oriented or mechanical the direction is, the director intends for the actor to produce something truthful. The adjustment must *always* be organic, and in order to achieve that, the character (not the actor) has to make the adjustment. Character decisions are the only acting decisions you should ever make, and character choices provide myriad options, even when the adjustment has to be made quickly. Here are a few examples:

1. "Make it faster."
   You are very excited.
   You have an urgent need to impart information.
   You have an important appointment in ten minutes.
   You are very fearful.

2. "Make it slower."
   You need to make every point perfectly clear.
   You feel uncomfortable about discussing it.

You are not feeling well.
You haven't fully thought it out yet.

3. "Make it bigger."
   You are losing your patience.
   You are overjoyed.
   The other characters are very young.
   The other characters are very old.

4. "Make it smaller."
   The situation is intimate.
   The information is confidential.
   The room is small.
   You are engaged in deception.

5. "Make it louder."
   There is a lot of background noise.
   What you have to say is very important.
   The other characters aren't paying attention.
   You are drunk.

6. "Make it quieter."
   You are ashamed of what you are saying.
   You don't want to attract attention.
   You are forbidden to speak.
   You are ill or dying.

If you have studied the material using Subjective Situation Perception, your character's options will be clear. The character will be able to respond quickly to even the most mechanical direction, and the results will be truthful and surprising.

■ *What is a line reading, and what purpose does it serve?*

A line reading is the recitation of a line of dialogue by a director, teacher or coach for the purpose of eliciting identical word emphasis from an actor. The assumption is, of course, that this *mechanical* directorial or teaching approach will effectively demonstrate the meaning of the line and that the actor will make sense out of it. That premise is not necessarily correct.

The problem inherent in line readings is the possibility that the actor will imitate the example but not understand the thought behind it. Acting is not mechanical. While it might be possible to achieve a seemingly truthful moment with a mechanical direction, the more likely result will be something transparently fake.

■ *What is a "thought reading"?*

A "thought reading" is a director's, coach's or teacher's direction of an actor by reading the line of dialogue (sometimes without the scripted words) to the actor in order to demonstrate the character's intention, instead of reading the line to demonstrate emphasis on a particular word or words. The effectiveness of this directorial (or teaching) approach depends on the acting and/or communicating ability of the director, coach or teacher. A clearly communicated thought reading will *always* produce a superior performance of that line to a clearly communicated line reading because the basis of a thought reading is truthful, whereas the basis of a line reading is mechanical.

■ *Will a director ever direct me in a language I don't understand, and is there a reliable way to deal with that situation?*

Someone will speak to you in your own language, but it might not be the director. The disconcerting part of communicating through an intermediary such as an assistant director or production assistant is the uncertainty that the dialogue between you and the director is being communicated word for word. In fact, you can be pretty sure that it won't be word for word, so just accept it and deal with it.

In *Lost in Translation*, directed by Sofia Coppola (whose screen-play won the Academy Award), Bill Murray's character is bewildered by the brevity of a production assistant's interpretation of a lengthy, impassioned, animated monologue from his Japanese director. The assistant's direction is, "Can you be more intense?" To which Bill Murray replies, "Is that all he said?"

The moment was especially funny to me because I had an identical experience working on *Lady Liberty*. Much of Mario Monicelli's direction was extensive but, unfortunately, all in Italian. By the time what I believed to be detailed information was distilled into English by Carlo Vanzina, the first assistant director (who has since become a prolific writer and director of Italian features), what I received was, "Mr. Monicelli wants you to stand closer to the desk," and, "Mr. Monicelli likes your face." The curiosity of that situation was that Mario directed the looping session in perfect and elegant English. Why he didn't speak to me in English on the set is just one of those mysteries that will have to remain unsolved.

■ *Is the stage director always in charge of final creative decisions?*

Yes, in all but extremely unusual circumstances (although considerable collaboration occurs along the way), the director of a stage production always has the final word. When those rare exceptions happen (and the director doesn't leave the production), the most likely cause is that the star (for whatever reason) needs to exercise power over some aspect of the proceedings, sometimes including the hiring and firing of other actors. It rarely improves a play when the director becomes subservient to other forces.

Regardless of production politics and intrigues, the message for actors in theatre, as in every other kind of work situation, is always the same: "Stay out of it. Just do your job."

■ *Is the movie director always in charge of final creative decisions?*

Not always. But he (or she) should be. An actor who is not the director of the film should never be in charge of a set or a production, no matter how big a star he or she may be. Even producers should leave the artistic business of the picture to the person they hired to direct it — or they should replace the director with a director they trust.

Movie stars are very careful about which directors they work with, not only because they like the director's work, but also because they know that if the star and the director ever disagree, the director will be strong enough to make the final decision and to stand up for the integrity of the production. If someone other than the director is allowed to make the creative decisions, the atmosphere on the set can be unsettling and the production often suffers.

If a film is released to bad notices or poor business, obviously the reputations and income of the director, the producer and the star are affected. When the movie turns out badly because the director's authority was usurped, everybody connected with the film loses something, and there is absolutely no excuse for it.

Regardless of the politics of the set, the actor has his own work to do. The unpredictability of the production elements that surround the actor makes it imperative that the actor protect himself from negative situations. The best way to accomplish that is by immersing himself in the character's life and staying focused on that task.

■ *Is the television director always in charge of final creative decisions?*

Directors of television movies usually are in charge of final creative decisions on the set, although in all television production many other "creative" (studio and network) opinions may rule the day after principal photography has been completed. In episodic television, the director of a drama is usually in charge, although there is considerable producer input. Comedy directors are frequently subservient to the producers or writers, and the director is usually subject to a great deal of producer watchfulness.

If the television director is not the one in charge, the true creative situation becomes very apparent very quickly. The actor has to do his own work regardless of who the boss is, and that should be of no concern to the actor. The television actor has to accept as a fact of life that he might find himself being directed by someone other than the director, including producers, writers and even the star of the show.

■ *What should I do if the other actors aren't good, are unprepared or misbehave in some way?*

You need to do nothing. The character can handle it. You are not required to react in any way to anything that occurs in the life of another actor (unless it has some tangible effect on your life or your well-being). In fact, you should have no opinions at all about anything you observe or hear about in a work situation (except when health and safety are at risk).

In almost every production, there are some people who seem to thrive on gossip, creating it, listening to it and spreading it. Distance yourself from those people and those occurrences. Don't even comment on things that you observe. All that discord diverts your attention and your energy from your job.

Several years ago, I arrived on a distant film location only to be informed that there might be some delays due to the misbehavior of one of the stars. It was apparent that the actor had suffered a mental episode that caused some bizarre behavior, which included striking a wardrobe person and hiding under a bus. Yet, when I met the actor I found him to be cordial, respectful, cooperative and professional in every way. I expected no less, and I got what I expected. There were no delays. Expectation is a form of rehearsal. Don't rehearse a result that you don't desire.

Regarding the preparedness or ability of other actors, don't give it a thought. If the actor is unprepared enough, he will be fired. If not, your character will see and hear what's going on and will respond appropriately to whatever he encounters.

■ *Does the process of discovery end with homework?*

Absolutely not. The actor's quest for completeness of character is only one aspect of discovery, which is, of course, essential to the work. No character is ever who he *seems* to be, because seeming is recognizing something seen before and expecting it to be repeated. The expectation of something recognizable lures actors into stereotypical repetitions, denying the inherent uniqueness that exists in every character. *Every preconception of character is a misconception.* So, in homework the character needs to be discovered.

But moments also have to be discovered. The *character* discovers brand new information on every page of every scene, which must be a continuous process throughout every performance. It is that vital discovery process which demonstrates the truthfulness in the newness of the character's life experiences. Without the surprises of discovery, the character wouldn't be a real person, and the performance would have been left at home.

■ *How do you work on a part you've been hired to play, but didn't audition for?*

Be extremely diligent. Being hired without an audition is a rare gift to an actor, and the actor needs to handle that gift with very great care. There are many obvious positive aspects to getting the part you didn't have to read for, most especially, just getting the job without the pressure of auditioning (and, in addition, getting a job that you may not have even known was being cast).

Unfortunately, there are some unsettling aspects, as well, for many actors who find themselves on the seemingly enviable receiving end of gift employment. What some actors find most daunting is the fact that the director has never heard him speak the lines and has no certainty of how he will play the part. In many instances, the actor hasn't even met the director and knows nothing of the director's personality or his working relationship with actors.

When I did *The Electric Horseman*, my first meeting with director Sydney Pollack was on the film's set at Caesar's Palace in Las Vegas, weeks after I had been hired. To go to work on *The Ice Runner*, I had traveled to the Soviet Union before I met the film's producer, Jeffrey Sneller, and its eventual director, Barry Samson. In fact, until I arrived in Moscow, I had never met anyone connected to the film. In every instance in which I was hired without auditioning, the director knew that I would show up prepared to do the work. The circumstances of the hiring may change, but the demands and the expectations are always the same.

Whether the actor is hired by auditioning, or as a result of a meeting with the director or producer or because of some aspect of his reputation, the director has (and must have) total confidence in the actor's ability to play the part better than any other actor he might have hired. It is the actor's responsibility to prove that the director's judgment was correct.

Fear is a great debilitator. When you are hired without an audition, you must approach the work with even greater dedication and focus than would otherwise be necessary in order to overcome every fearful concern. If you have done your homework, the director's expectations will be met and exceeded. And, in practice, that is almost always the case. You can help your own mental state by knowing that when you are hired, it is never a mistake. The only mistake producers and directors make is the hiring of someone else.

■ *What do you mean by "collaborative cooperation"?*

The actor's work isn't solitary. He relies on the efforts of many other professionals in a variety of disciplines (besides the obvious contributions of other actors, the writer and the director) in order to do his best work and to have it presented in the most truthful and interesting way.

In stage production, costumes, props, scenery, lighting and sound effects all have an impact on the actor and his ability to concentrate most efficiently on his own work, as well as on the performance the audience sees. In film and television, there are the additional vitally important areas of cinematography, film editing and even the makeup department.

Particularly in film and television, the contribution of each professional is so important to the total effort that it may determine how every other person's work is seen, how much of it is seen and maybe even whether or not it is seen at all. For some reason, actors in general seem less cognizant than they ought to be of the valuable input of others into the ultimate effectiveness of their acting efforts. But the best, most experienced actors make use of everything remotely connected to their own work, and, as a result, entire productions are invariably enhanced.

■ *When do actors have to do their own makeup?*

Actors almost always need to provide and apply their own makeup for plays. In film and television (and commercials), professional makeup artists are provided by the production companies.

An actor in a play needs to know his makeup requirements before the first dress rehearsal, and he needs to have as much of it as he needs for each performance. He has to have some expertise in the application of makeup, which requires class work, experimentation, practice and research. Actors should not expect other actors to supply their makeup nor to apply it for them.

Professional makeup artists are highly skilled, and their approach to the makeup on any particular film or television show has been designed (in the course of production meetings) to complement the director's and producer's vision, as well as the style and tone of the production, the cinematographer's lighting demands and climatic conditions.

Unless the makeup artist asks for the actor's opinions or suggestions, the actor should refrain from offering them, unless there is important information that only the actor knows. It would be helpful for the makeup artist to know that the actor's skin is very oily, that he perspires heavily or that he has allergic reactions to certain kinds of makeup. Valid character suggestions (in collaboration with the director) such as scars and other blemishes are usually welcomed because they acknowledge and highlight the makeup artist's contribution to the production.

It is the actor's responsibility to keep makeup off the wardrobe and props, unless the action of the show makes that impossible. If the actor knows that his makeup has strayed onto his (or another actor's) wardrobe, he has to immediately call the problem to the attention of the wardrobe department. It is another part of the necessity for being focused on the work and engaged in every aspect of it.

■ *How much input is an actor allowed to have when it comes to things like props and wardrobe?*

Actually, generally speaking, an actor's ideas about things that directly concern the character are usually welcomed, particularly when they make sense and they are presented in a helpful, nonassertive (nobody likes to feel as if their expertise is being challenged) way.

In my own experience, costume designers often ask how I would like a particular garment cut or altered or if I would prefer one garment over another. Usually, wardrobe professionals come up with wonderful concepts and selections, and when I have no preference, I just compliment them on their work and say that whatever they choose will be fine. When I have wardrobe ideas, which are always based on character considerations, those preferences have invariably been honored.

Actors need to learn about *every* unfamiliar aspect of the wardrobe they will wear in a production, particularly period wardrobe. Even though the costume designer may be extremely knowledgeable (and they generally are), the actor still must learn how garments are *lived in* by those who wear them in their daily lives. Photographs, paintings and good contemporaneous writings are excellent sources of that information.

Emmy-nominated costume designer Marcy Froehlich recalls that when she was assistant designer to two-time Academy Award-winning costume designer Albert Wolsky (*All that Jazz* and *Bugsy*) on *Road to Perdition*, Jude Law made his wardrobe fitting *a character experience*. He gave *the character* the opportunity to feel and test the appropriateness of every garment. Marcy says the experience made a positive and memorable impression on her. Her vivid and favorable recollection should remind and inspire every actor to use his own wardrobe calls as an extension of his character homework.

Property masters, like costumers, usually welcome reasonable and interesting character-based prop suggestions (and contributions). The actor's own jewelry and small practical items (cameras, cigar cutters, pocket magnifiers, etc.), if the period and style are appropriate, are especially good because the character can easily become comfortable with them. It is impossible to predict, however, how the actor's prop choices, no matter how appropriate or well researched, will be received.

In *Columbo,* my character Jason Danziger theorized that the murder victim was actually a suicide who used an "elastic tether" to shoot himself twice and then dispose of the weapon, so I asked the prop department for some elastic so that Danziger could demonstrate his goofy theory. My request was happily satisfied because it made sense and provided an opportunity for props to enhance the production.

When I did *Comes a Horseman*, however, my prop contributions received mixed results. Props was delighted with my period eyeglasses, but my geologist's magnifier didn't make it past director Alan J. Pakula's vigilant scrutiny. The conversation went like this. "Basil, why are you wearing that whistle around your neck?" "Alan, it's a magnifying glass. Geologists in the field all wear them." "It looks like a whistle. Don't wear it." Of course, Alan was right. It did look like a whistle. Authentic or not, it would have been distracting to any audience member (unless he happened to be a geologist) who noticed it.

Actors should be warned that when it comes to personal items (wardrobe and props) used in film or television, the production company will retain custody of the items, sometimes until the entire production has wrapped, because of the necessity of guaranteeing a match whenever the character's appearance requires that article of apparel or jewelry.

The *selection* of appropriate wardrobe and props is only the initial baby step in dressing and propping the character. The actor's *use* of the garment or object must be perfectly appropriate to the *character's* comfort and familiarity with it.

Three examples come immediately to mind in which the actors were so adept in their required use of props that their characters *seemed* to be the experts that the text indicated them to be. Academy Award winner (for *Hamlet*) Sir Laurence Olivier's Nazi dentist in

Marathon Man, Nick Nolte's news photographer in *Under Fire* and two-time Academy Award winner (in *Kramer vs. Kramer* and *Sophie's Choice*) Meryl Streep's violin teacher in *Music of the Heart* are such textbook demonstrations of actors fulfilling the scripts' technical demands on their characters that every actor can be inspired by them.

There is, of course, the opposite situation, in which a *character* is so unfamiliar or uncomfortable in the use of a prop that his resulting behavior is truthfully awkward. In *The Electric Horseman*, Sonny, played by Robert Redford, borrows a pair of sunglasses from Jane Fonda's character, Hallie. Unfortunately for Sonny, they are prescription sunglasses and he can't see clearly when he's wearing them, but he can't take them off, for fear of being recognized. The moments that result are subtle, truthful and very funny, because Robert Redford had mastered his character's *inability* to make the prop work.

Actors must know that natural expertness with garments, hand props, furniture and scenery (doors, windows, flagpoles, etc.) that the character has used and lived with for years may require expert instruction and many hours of repetitive practice to master. The actor must spend as much time as necessary to achieve that level of expertise and not one minute less.

Great acting doesn't occur magically or through some accidental gift of fate. Meryl Streep might have spent many weeks in violin practice with a qualified coach just to master the use of a single prop. *Whether it took her five hours or five months is irrelevant. She took as long as was necessary to convincingly play the part.*

For an actor to begin to work with a technical and unfamiliar prop ten minutes before his first rehearsal requiring use of the prop would be foolish and inappropriate. Furthermore, that lack of adequate preparation would be extremely costly to the production because of the time and effort required to fire the actor and hire and rehearse someone else.

■ *Should the actor deal directly with the cinematographer, and how might that affect his performance?*

The actor must have conversation with the cinematographer (DP or director of photography) or the camera operator on every "single" (only one actor in the picture) shot to find out the *specific* size of the frame (extreme close-up, medium close-up, etc.). The actor always needs to know if camera requirements will limit his physicality (head movement, gestures, etc.). The actor's lack of information can necessitate costly retakes, when a simple question like "How much of me is in this shot?" would have prevented the problem.

Besides being professional courtesy, establishing a good working relationship with the cinematographer might actually have tangible job benefits as well. On two such occasions, feature cinematographers with whom I had worked hired me for commercials they were directing. Robbie Greenberg, whom I worked with on Robert Redford's *The Milagro Beanfield War*, cast me in an Oldsmobile commercial. Five-time Academy Award-nominated cinematographer Owen Roizman, who had been DP on *The Electric Horseman* for Sydney Pollack, hired me for an Anheuser Busch Natural Light Beer commercial with Norm Crosby that turned into a series of commercials for me. Would they have hired me even if we hadn't worked together? Maybe. But maybe not.

I also had the extreme good fortune to be directed by two Academy Award-winning cinematographers with whom I had not worked before, Haskell Wexler (*Who's Afraid of Virginia Woolf* and *Bound for Glory*) in a commercial for Prestone II, and Guy Green (*Great Expectations*) in a television movie, *Jennifer: A Woman's Story*, starring Elizabeth Montgomery.

■ *What effect does the film editor have on an actor's*
performance, and does the actor have direct contact
with the editor?

The film editor has no effect on the actor's performance on the set,
but has complete control (with the director, of course) over the performance that ultimately reaches the screen.

Actors have no way of knowing which takes will wind up in the
film or whether or not any particular take will even be printed. When
the director perceives during shooting that some element of the scene
is unsatisfactory, he calls for a retake, so that piece of film doesn't
even reach the cutting room, much less the cutting room floor (since
the advent of computer technology, films are no longer cut and
assembled as they were when the terms cutting room and cutting
room floor had literal meanings, but you get the idea).

After the scene has been shot (and screened in dailies) and the
printed takes get into the hands of the editor, composition decisions
begin to be made. *Even though the director and the editor are in con-*
trol of the selection process, the actor actually determines the qual-
ity of his work that gets into the theatres or onto the television screen.

There are many reasons why a particular shot is or is not printed,
but the choice may have nothing to do with your performance. To
ensure that your best performance gets to the editor, just do your best
work in every take. It's that simple.

If, however, your acting is better in one take than in another, one
moment of carelessness might sabotage your own best work. Sometimes the director, script supervisor, cinematographer, property master, set decorator, makeup artist, hairdresser and all the assistants will
miss something important that only becomes obvious when viewed
without distraction in the editing room. And when that happens,
quality of the acting becomes secondary to the coherence of the film.
If the offensive element (a plastic cup in President Lincoln's office,
lipstick that suddenly appears on an actress's lips in the middle of a

scene, etc.) can be eliminated by choosing another take of the same moment, then the actor's work in that particular take, good or not, will never be seen. If another, unmarred take of that actor in that setup can be used, the actor is very fortunate. If there is no other printed take available, the only option might be for the editor to choose a different or reverse angle, eliminating the on-camera appearances of all the actors in the unusable shot — or, the moment, if not indispensable to the film, might be eliminated entirely.

There will be times when the editor needs the shot because no coverage exists and the director needs the moment. When that happens, and it is rare, the actor gets his work on the screen, but the distracting gaffe is still there. A striking example of an apparently indispensable piece of film, blemish included, appears in the British film *Clouds Over Europe*. In that scene, the great actor Sir Ralph Richardson wears a white pocket square leaving one room, walks through a doorway, and isn't wearing it when he emerges into the next room. A minute later, he is shown seated with the handkerchief again neatly in place. If the director hadn't really needed it, the shot minus the handkerchief would have been edited out. Any actor (even a star) who allows a gross mismatch in his own performance (including makeup, props and wardrobe) has only himself to blame if his on-camera work is edited out of the scene. Help the editor (and the director and yourself) by being attentive to the details.

On many feature films, the editor or editors spend a considerable amount of time on the set. Getting to know them can be helpful. On *All the President's Men*, one of the editors, Tim O'Meara, provided me with a piece of film that I was able to use as a publicity photo. Furthermore, editors sometimes become directors. Academy Award winner Robert Wise (*West Side Story* and *The Sound of Music*), for example, had been an editor on *Citizen Kane, The Hunchback of Notre Dame* and many other important pictures. It is impossible to anticipate the rewards that may accrue to an actor from high standards of professionalism in interacting with everyone on the set.

■ *What is A.D.R.?*

A.D.R. is automated dialogue replacement, also called looping or dubbing. Its purpose is the production of "clean" dialogue to replace unclear, overlapped or otherwise unusable dialogue on the originally recorded soundtrack or to create dialogue not included on the original track.

Looping sessions are performed on recording stages (soundproof studios) on which the actor, after hearing a series of warning beeps, speaks the lines into a microphone as he watches himself (or some other actor) speaking on the film. The process is repeated over and over again in very short pieces (loops), until the loop has been satisfactorily matched in both sound and intensity to the lip movements on the screen. Only when the session director is satisfied that the match is perfect does he move on to the next loop.

Every actor who works in film will be called upon to loop dialogue at some point. Actors who dread (or fear) the mechanics of the process don't adapt to looping as well as actors who approach it as enthusiastically and painstakingly as they do the on-camera work. A good dubbing actor can actually improve an onscreen performance.

■ *How do you deal with being fired?*

There is no good (painless) way that I know of. Doing the best work you can at all times is the only way to approach the job. Being fired (like being hired) is a decision over which the actor has no control. *Every* actor who has been in the business for very long has been fired or replaced on some job, somewhere, sometime. I was replaced in a show in *acting school*. You just have to get over it and move on. It's not the end of the world. It's not even the end of the career.

Then there are times when you just see it coming (on a subconscious level, most actors fear that they may be fired at any time). I had one of those experiences on the set of the television show, *Bar-*

ney Miller. We had finished our first cast reading (called the table reading), and we were on a short break, when the stage manager Jeff Melman (who later became quite a successful director) came to me with a message. "Danny (the creator and executive producer Danny Arnold) wants to see you in his office." I started to get up from the table and Jeff added, "And you can take your things." It was one of those dark moments when you know that what's coming won't be good. So I went to Danny's office (with my things). But I wasn't fired. The show was too long, so they had to cut something and that turned out to be my scene. The good news was that my character would be written into a subsequent episode (which it was, so that I was paid for an additional week).

There are the times when an actor is cut out of a show and that is the end of it. It happens to everyone. But don't anticipate it. Never rehearse a result that you don't desire. Firings are rare and they almost never have anything to do with the actor's work. Just do what you do and don't give it a thought. *Don't give it a thought.*

VIII. COMMERCIALS ▪

TELEVISION COMMERCIALS have provided many actors, myself included, high profile entree into the lucrative side of the acting profession. Actors with meager resumes and no reputation often find very limited access to most of the paying jobs in plays, film and television in New York and Los Angeles. That is not the case for many of those same actors when it comes to television commercials.

Commercials are not theatrical feature films, and they are not television shows. Although there is some entertainment value in many commercials, entertainment is not the goal of the advertiser. His goal is advertisement for the purpose of selling his product or service. It is important for actors to accept the needs and methods of the advertising industry and adapt to them when they pursue commercial work so that they don't assume inappropriate attitudes when confronted with the norms of that industry.

The use of actors in commercials is only one facet of an advertiser's total marketing campaign, and a relatively recent one at that. Before commercials, there was only print advertising, which included newspapers, magazines, billboards, product labels and point-of-purchase, and the people who appeared in advertisements were models. Models were hired by the advertising agencies on the basis of their photo portfolios and personal interviews.

When commercials began, the advertising agencies continued to hire the talent, who were still, for the most part, models, except for the spokesmen who came from radio. Eventually, commercials needed actors, so the advertising agencies opened casting departments and the heads of some of those departments were former well-known radio actors like Sybil Trent and Rollie Bestor. For many years, particularly in New York, all commercial casting was done at the ad agencies — and, even until the 1970s, commercial actors in Hollywood were required to use model-type composite four-different-poses-on-a-page photographs, even though the practice had long been abandoned in New York in favor of actors' head shots. Until recent years, auditions for commercials in Hollywood were still referred to as "interviews," a throwback to the days when commercials were peopled by models.

Since those days, however, the commercial industry, as it relates to actors, has evolved. Very little on-camera casting is now done at advertising agencies, and most casting directors are independents, some of whom cast film and television, as well. It almost goes without saying that many established and even star actors now regularly perform commercial work. But that was not always the case.

In the past, it seemed fashionable in some acting circles, particularly in New York, to view commercials as an unworthy pursuit for serious actors. That attitude lost credibility decades ago when distinguished actors of the caliber of Sir Laurence Olivier, for Polaroid, and another Academy Award winner, Henry Fonda (*On Golden Pond*), for GAF, bridged the respectability gap, ending that nonsense forever. Today, the only actors to whom commercial acting is somehow distasteful are the actors who can't get those jobs (or who no longer need the money and have tired of the process).

Commercials are an important, generally accessible source of lucrative income for actors. The resulting boost to an actor's self esteem, lifestyle and overall well-being provided by commercial income can be significant. Furthermore, when actors achieve some financial stability without the necessity of maintaining full-time, non-acting jobs, they can more fully engage in the necessities of career building. Commercials also afford actors some worthwhile exposure to important film and television people in New York and Los Angeles, and there have been instances in which one commercial role has opened the door to meaningful jobs in film and television.

Even though essential acting principles never change, there are a few unique aspects of the commercial business that actors should understand and appreciate. This chapter addresses those differences.

■ *How do actors get auditions for commercials?*

Unlike the casting criteria for movie and television roles, commercial casting relies almost exclusively on character type, with less attention paid to credits and experience. For that reason, commercial auditions are accessible to every actor who makes a concerted effort to enter the field. However, also unlike films, television, and plays, the casting of commercials is not open to direct submissions by actors, so commercial agents are necessary.

Even though many more actors are likely to be auditioned for most commercial roles than for most non-commercial roles, there is always some finite number of actors who will be seen. The actor who is known (in a positive way) by the casting director has the best possibility of being on an audition list. Therefore, actors should make every effort to contact and meet the commercial casting directors (a few of whom cast films and television, as well). That being said, the actor still needs to have a *good* commercial agent.

There are scores of reputable agents in New York and Los Angeles who represent actors for commercial work. However, being reputable and being good are not necessarily the same thing.

The only good agent is an agent who is effective. The most *potentially* effective commercial agents are those who get *all* the casting calls, and there are probably fewer than a dozen of those on each coast (New York and Los Angeles).

There are only three ways of finding out who those agents are. One excellent way to get those names is by asking very successful commercial actors who represents them. But that method presupposes that you know a lot of those actors.

The fastest way to get those agency names is by asking major casting directors which agents they call *every* time they cast (if they will give you that information).

The other method of identifying those agents is to observe the recognizability of their clients, and there is a reliable way to do that. The *Players Directory* in Los Angeles publishes pictures and representation information on virtually every working actor in the business. The Academy of Motion Picture Arts and Sciences Library has current editions available for inspection. The agents who represent the most recognizable faces are the agents who get all the calls. It is important for you to know that the agent lists provided by Screen Actors Guild are not all-inclusive, and some of the most prominent agents aren't on those lists.

The most important introduction to a good agent is a good picture. Your picture must show your most castable quality, meaning that it needs to make clear (to the least imaginative person in the world) how many commercials you are appropriate for. And your picture must look *exactly* the way you look, *only better*. Even though many agents will ask for new and different kinds of photos, you still need good photos to get the agent, so you have to make that necessary investment. Every photographer is eager to show his portfolio, so make as many comparisons (of product, personality, and price) as you need to before you spend the money.

■ *Do commercials make demands on the actor that are different from the demands of stage and screen work?*

In some ways, yes. And those differences begin with the first audition. There are also differences in the shooting process, and there are even differences for the actor after principal photography has been completed.

Under usual circumstances, the audition experience in commercials is unlike what the actor will encounter anywhere else in the business. In the first place, waiting rooms are often *packed* with actors because the industry's casting personnel, including producers and directors, can no longer make decisions unless they audition a lot of actors (many of whom are not actors, but just people from other professions, or no professions, who found out there is a lot of money being made in commercials). Except for the crowded waiting rooms (which any actor should be happy to be part of since these are work opportunities), most of the other commercial audition peculiarities are helpful to the actor.

The availability and the thoroughness of material offered to the auditioning actor in commercials exceeds what is generally available to actors reading for theatrical (including film and television) work. Story boards and complete scripts are almost always provided.

From the very beginning, the commercial audition itself is also a different experience, and the actor can use the opening moments to considerable advantage. The first thing the actor is asked to do on camera is to "slate," which means to identify himself, usually just by saying his name. The actor can use the slate to truthfully and energetically establish character, purpose, and feelings. By starting his performance in that opening moment, the actor actually begins his audition without ever being seen out of character, before the director has even an instant to preconceive anything about him.

Before the audition begins and at various points during the audition, every actor receives detailed instruction covering every nuance of performance. This moment-by-moment direction conveys the director's desires as interpreted by the casting director and the camera operator, and much of it is very helpful. The talent in commercials is secondary to the picture, because of the specificity of the advertiser's message and the very short amount of time available to present it. Therefore, the actor has to fit into the strictly predetermined format *and still be interesting and truthful*. So it is important for the actor to know the director's plan for every moment of his commercial.

On the commercial set, there are two major differences for the actor from other kinds of work in film. One important distinction is the amount of film that is shot. Typically, one thirty or sixty-second commercial takes one full day or longer to film. Actors are usually required to shoot more takes, sometimes necessitated by critical timing demands. The second significant convention that is unique to commercial filming is the presence of many "directors" on some commercial sets. Those "directors" are the advertising and client representatives who are sometimes allowed to offer unsolicited creative suggestions to the director and the actors. Most good directors control the shoot so that extraneous interference doesn't occur. But when it is allowed, even through the silly suggestions, extra takes and lengthened work days, the actor should be cheerful and the acting must still be interesting and truthful.

Finally, after principal photography is completed, there is one more important difference for actors in commercials as opposed to other kinds of film work. If the actor requests it, the advertising agency will usually give him a copy of the completed commercial, at no charge, sometimes on 35-millimeter film, but most often on DVD. In addition to the gainful employment provided, sometimes for a lot of money, the free footage is one of the classier aspects of the commercial industry.

IX. CAREER MANAGEMENT ⋮

MORE THAN TWENTY YEARS AGO, I started to write my first book, as yet unpublished (and unfinished), entitled *The Acting Business and How to Be Good at It.* The intended purpose of that initial writing effort was (and still is) the introduction of sound business principles to professional actors and the development of those principles into a coherent and systematic businesslike approach (and attitude) in the pursuit of success.

Building a career in the acting business isn't easy. But neither is anything else that pays this well. The good news is that it also isn't complicated. Hard work is necessary to achieve success as an actor. But even though a good work ethic is an admirable and vital attribute, *unfocused* hard work is a waste of valuable time. No one who is willing to work hard to become a good actor, with the intention of being consistently, gainfully employed in the profession, should fail because the employment part was mysterious and seemingly inaccessible.

Success begins in the mind. Actors need to see themselves as *successful* actors. It is a natural state of mind that *always* precedes the decision to become an actor. It's part of the dream. Unfortunately, however, beginning actors don't usually have access to the personal influence of those who have succeeded. But they have great access and constant contact with many who have failed and who reek of low expectations (of themselves and of others), resentment and bitterness. To achieve success, actors need to nurture the high hopes that drew them to this profession, and they can best do that by learning the fundamentals of the acting *business*. And they need to aggressively remove themselves from all those who traffic in failure.

From my initial enlightenment in the non-accidental aspects of acting employment, I have felt empowered and in control of my own fortunes in this business. The principles that I learned are not uniquely applicable to me and my career. They work for everyone who applies them. Actors who make the substantial commitment of time, money, emotional energy and plain old hard work necessary to achieve proficiency in the craft of acting *deserve* to be rewarded in the professional practice of that craft. Herein are the concepts and specific activities that I recommend to every actor who wants to proactively determine the best and most profitable course of his own career.

■ *What necessities should an actor acquire as he pursues a career?*

Proper training and information are vital. One is useless without the other. Training is necessary so that the actor can successfully practice his craft. Information is necessary so that the actor can most effectively and truthfully play a role and so that he can learn everything he needs to know about the *business*.

■ *What is "thinking in the profession"?*

An actor who thinks in the profession is *always* aware of things, business and social, that may have some effect on his career. It might be observations that will improve his craft. It might be the receipt of information that can lead to a job. It might be an opportunity to offer meaningful help to someone else in the business, even though there is no immediate prospect for his own reward. Many successful professional actors have this awareness. I am surprised that some don't.

■ *Are there any guidelines for starting and maintaining an acting career?*

There are logical, common sense ideas that every actor should at least consider in pursuit of an acting career. Here is a short list of some of the necessities:

1. Establish your long-term goal, in terms of the *kind* of career you are striving for. For example, the goal may be to play leading roles in Broadway plays. It may be to play leading roles in Broadway musicals, or in repertory companies, or in feature films — or to play a regular role in a television soap opera or a primetime series. It is the long-term goal that determines your training choices and where you go to pursue your career.

2. Determine what short-term goal will best lead you to your long-term goal. Getting an acting job is *always* the short-term goal — and there is always more than one job or kind of job that will move you along the path toward the career you want. If your long-term goal is to play leading roles in feature films, either a television commercial or an off-Broadway play would be suitable jobs on the way up that ladder. Getting a good acting teacher, photographer, agent, manager, Equity-waiver play or student film are not short-term goals; they are means for reaching your goals. *Your short-term goal is a job. Stay focused on work.*

3. Write up your business plan. The business plan should include your goals and *everything* you will need to do and to get in order to attain those goals, including finding a suitable place to live, establishing an income, developing and maintaining necessary skills, acquiring vital business tools (including photos and trade papers), preparing and maintaining comprehensive business contact records, developing an ongoing prioritized

daily plan (including all career-related activities), finding and reaching prospective employers (casting directors and producers) and hiring employees and associates (agents, managers, publicists, business managers, lawyers, etc.) when necessary.

4. Be flexible enough to adjust your goals as your skills, interests and career change, but *never* lower your long-term goal. Never, never, never become discouraged. Become more pro-active instead. Acting success can happen at any time. Two of the most important and famous character actors in the history of American films, Sidney Greenstreet and Academy Award winner Charles Coburn (*The More the Merrier*), *began* prolific movie careers at a time when many people think of retiring, Coburn at 55 and Greenstreet at 62.

5. Learn as much as you can about the current work being done in theatre, film and television. And learn some history, particularly about actors and directors, whose films are easily accessible. You must know about the important achievements that were made before the day you decided to enter the business.

■ *What are actors' most serious career mistakes?*

There are ten common, serious mistakes made by aspiring and even experienced actors. Failure to avoid any one of these mistakes can prevent a meaningful career from ever getting started. An established career can be damaged or ended by inattention to these important principles. For those reasons, I regard each of these potential mistakes as extremely serious. Here is my list of the ten most serious career mistakes an actor can make.

1. Neglecting the craft.
   Not even the most powerful managers and press agents can long overcome an actor's inability to develop and maintain

sound, reliable professional acting skills. Actors are not required to be versatile. But every actor *must* be very, very good at playing some roles and *must know* what those roles are. You must not allow inactivity or fear to erode either your ability or your confidence.

2. Leaving the career in the hands of others.

3. Believing that success will come by waiting for it.

4. Expecting too much too fast.

5. Not learning and practicing essential, common sense social and business skills. Fundamental in this is the necessity for circumspection in the dissemination of your own positive career information to people who have no *need* for that information. Reporting successes of *any* kind (agent meetings and signings, auditions, jobs, etc.) at any stage of your career to other actors (and former actors), regardless of their achievements or their relationship to you, is an extremely bad idea. It will never produce a positive result, and the negative possibilities are greater than you may imagine. Don't do it.

6. Failure to consistently adhere to the four essentials of professionalism—promptness, preparedness, propriety and principle.

7. Refusal to pay for essential training and failing to use common sense and reasonable research in selecting schools, teachers and coaches.

8. Refusal to pay for important career enhancement, and making poor comparative, cost-effective and time-effective choices in selecting those career enhancement opportunities. Included in this category would be such items as agents, managers, photographers and casting director and agent workshops and showcases.

9. Failure to develop and adhere to a training plan and a business plan.

10. Failure to demonstrate honesty, kindness and gratitude, and associating with people who are not honest, kind and grateful.

■ *What do star actors have in common?*

They are very disciplined and they work extremely hard. Furthermore, they are driven to succeed and they will not be deterred from reaching that goal. There are *no* exceptions to this rule.

Talent has always been and always will be an unreliable predictor of success, because it is a completely subjective concept that usually refers to some innate ability and is not applicable to anything in the real world, except for the praise it engenders from family, friends and some teachers. There are countless legions of "talented" classroom award winners who fail to achieve beyond the classroom. Conversely, there are numerous examples of long, distinguished careers established by actors who had been authoritatively pronounced inadequate.

The brilliant Sir Alec Guinness, one of the greatest actors of the twentieth century, had been discouraged, as a "talentless" young boy, from participation in dramatics by the headmaster of his Pembroke Lodge boarding school. He proceeded to the Fay Compton School of Acting where he was told by his teacher Martita Hunt that he had "absolutely no talent."

Bette Davis succeeded despite rejection by the celebrated Broadway star, repertory impresario and teacher Eva Le Gallienne and her subsequent dismissal from a stock company in Rochester, New York, by George Cukor (who later became an Academy Award-winning director for *My Fair Lady*).

The excellent Academy Award-nominated character actor Charles Durning wasn't talented enough to be invited to return for a second year at the American Academy of Dramatic Arts in New York, before going on to establish a long and distinguished stage and film career.

The list goes on and on. As screenwriter and novelist William Goldman stated repeatedly and so succinctly in his memoir, *Adventures in the Screen Trade*, "Nobody knows anything." Words to remember.

The acting profession doesn't care what the soon-to-be-forgotten or even the very-famous-and-well-respected judges of talent think or say about an actor's ability or his prospects. The profession rewards a relentless pursuit of success and the attainment of whatever skills are necessary to achieve that success. That has always been so and there will never be a different path to sustained stardom.

■ *Doesn't luck play some part in an actor's success?*

No. Actors don't serve themselves well by believing in luck, because that belief leads to unproductive resentments and ingratitude and to the neglect of important career-enhancing activities. Attributing another actor's success to luck is a demeaning intrusion into someone else's life, based on incomplete (or a complete lack of) information. By believing that some achievement or success came to you by luck eliminates any possibility that you might repeat the process that led to the success. If you believe that bad luck prevents your success, you won't be investigating and correcting the real problems.

What many people think of as good or bad luck is really the result of some conscious action or series of actions by the actor prior to the "lucky" or "unlucky" event. I know of "unlucky" instances in my own career that might have turned out to be "lucky" if only I had prepared better, or been a better listener to the still, small voice inside me or behaved differently. I have turned down jobs for foolish reasons and I have failed to follow up on situations that might have been work-producing opportunities. But by knowing that the outcomes were my own doing, I have been able to make some corrections.

There have been many, many instances in which good things came to me because of specific things I did, *even when I didn't know that those future good things even existed.* I will mention three of those situations because there is an important lesson in each of them.

Just a few years after I had arrived in Los Angeles, an actress friend, Alix Elias, asked me if I might be interested in a role in a short film being done by a directing student at the American Film Institute. It was a cute comedy with a very short shooting schedule (but no salary), so I did it. Two years later, that young director, Kim Friedman, asked me to read for a pilot she was shooting. I got the job, the series was picked up and I played the regular role of Principal Dingleman on the CBS series, *Square Pegs* (with some very talented young actresses, including Amy Linker, Tracy Nelson, Jami Gertz, and eventual multiple Emmy winner Sarah Jessica Parker).

One day I noticed a tiny press release in *The Hollywood Reporter*, notifying the industry that Doris Quinlan, whom I had worked for on *One Life to Live* in New York, had become a producer at Marble Arch Productions. I called Doris, visited her in her office, and was cast in a very good role in a television movie, *Jennifer: A Woman's Story*, directed by Academy Award-winning cinematographer Guy Green. Being a faithful reader of the trade papers (*Hollywood Reporter* and *Daily Variety*) from my very first day in California has paid off many times.

Alan Shayne, a prominent casting director whom I had met in New York, was casting feature films at Warner Brothers. My agent at that time was Tom Jennings, who had recently been a casting director at Warner Brothers and knew Alan very well. I told Tom that I needed to renew my acquaintance with Alan, so it was done and we had a brief meeting. The result was my meeting with Alan J. Pakula and a role in *All the President's Men*. That was my first of four films with Robert Redford and a relationship that has led, *directly* in many cases (including another picture for Alan Pakula, a major television miniseries, and four films for Academy Award-winning directors), to every good thing that has happened to my career in California.

The preceding events contain elements that might be attributed to luck, except that without my instigation the events would have never occurred. It is impossible to overemphasize the necessity of being in the right place at the right time, and every time I mention it, actors challenge my assertion that it is within their control. My response is always the same. "You have to be in a lot of places a lot of times."

■ Can one negative professional experience damage my career?

Probably not. You will be surprised to discover how quickly a traumatic moment can be made to disappear in the light of subsequent events. Shortly after I arrived in Hollywood, I embarked on a campaign to meet every important casting director in the industry. My efforts met with some immediate success, and I was beginning to get a lot of auditions for television and films. My commercial agent at the Jack Wormser Agency, and later my friend, Sandy Joseph, recommended me to the casting director (whose name I won't mention) who cast all the shows for Hollywood's most successful television comedy producer, Norman Lear (*All in the Family*, *Sanford and Son*, *The Jeffersons*, etc.). The casting director's response was, "Basil Hoffman! I never want to hear that name again."

When I was told about the casting director's comment, I was devastated. I had been taken out of contention for some of the best television work in town. Or so I thought.

Two weeks later, Redd Foxx, the star of *Sanford and Son*, fired that casting director from his show. NBC hired Reuben Cannon, a casting director at Universal Studios whom I had met, to cast the series and Reuben hired me to do the show. Over the next few years I did another episode of *Sanford and Son*, a movie, and the CBS television series *Square Pegs* for Norman Lear, the producer who I thought would never hire me because of one incident. I also was hired for an ABC television pilot, *My Buddy*, with Redd Foxx (at Redd's request).

I never found out why that casting director whom I had never met had a strong negative reaction to me. The important thing is that it didn't matter. If you won't be stopped, then nothing will stop you.

■ *Are there any special industry information sources that I should know about?*

There is a broad spectrum of helpful and reliable sources of industry information available in bookstores and on the Internet that service the acting community. Here are a few of them that I believe every actor should at least know about. Some of them will prove indispensable.

1. Trade Papers:

   Daily Variety and *The Hollywood Reporter*, published five days a week, are the industry bibles. They are filled with important film and television casting and pre-casting information, some in regular listings and some hidden in news stories and columns.

   Back Stage in New York and *Back Stage West* in Los Angeles, published weekly, are excellent sources of theatre casting information including Equity waiver plays, and they also include many casting notices for low budget and student films.

   Student films offer good opportunities for actors to get film experience (without pay), work with future important directors and compile material for their demo reels (although actors need to learn to objectively discriminate between what is a high standard of professional work and what is not and to only include on a reel the work that is up to that standard).

2. Books:

   Halliwell's Who's Who in the Movies, *Halliwell's Film Guide*, Ephraim Katz's *Film Encyclopedia* and *The American Film Institute Desk Reference* are worthwhile additions to every actor's library, although much of the information is also available online (but not necessarily in such organized form).

3. Internet:

   Screen Actors Guild (*sag.org*), AFTRA (*aftra.com*), Actors Equity Association (*actorsequity.org*), the Academy of Motion Picture Arts and Sciences (*oscars.org*), and the Academy of Television Arts and Sciences (*emmys.com*) have free Web sites with useful and sometimes vital information for actors.

   The Internet Movie Database (*imdb.com*), also free, is the industry standard for credit listings of every person who *ever* received onscreen credit for *any work* performed in a theatrical feature film or television program, listed by name of the person and by the title of the project. Unfortunately, the information is incomplete. Nevertheless, this is the best quick source available for learning who's who and what's what in the industry.

   Talent manager/publicist Brad Lemack's excellent actors' business textbook, *The Business of Acting*, is the centerpiece of *thebusinessofacting.com*, a free Web site that contains information and links designed to give actors easy access to some important tools of the trade.

   K Callan, an excellent actress with a long, successful and ongoing career, has written (and continually updates) a series of books for actors (and writers and directors) which offer career information and advice. Her material is especially valuable because it comes from a working actor's experience at the highest levels of the industry. Her books are available at most bookstores and on the Internet at *kcallan.com* and *swedenpress.com*.

NowCasting.com is one of the best, most cost-effective and must-use Web sites for actors, created and designed by actors, offering a wide variety of marketing, networking, submission and information services (many of them free) including actor profiles, audition sides and its weekly e-magazine, *Actors Ink*. The company is an industry leader in online demo reels and resume clips, pioneering the technology for online auditions for domestic and international casting. Now Casting publishes the comprehensive monthly *Casting Director Guide*, available at Samuel French bookstores in Los Angeles and included in some monthly memberships which also include online casting submissions. The *Players Directory*, the industry's casting bible for over seventy years, is published by Now Casting, and all its actor profiles, demo reels, and resume clips are automatically online at *PlayersDirectory.com* and Baseline StudioSystems (an industry database used by studios and executives).

L.A. Casting (*lacasting.com*) is the casting reference for the television commercial industry. It is absolutely necessary for every on-camera commercial actor to be represented on that site. This Web site is also a worthwhile movie and television casting resource.

Breakdown Services, Ltd. (the film, television and theatre casting resource used by every casting director) created and manages Actors Access (*actorsaccess.com*). This Web site is the actors' most reliable Internet connection to the casting industry. Every actor should have photos and a demo reel on that site. Actors Access also provides audition sides for virtually every film and television production cast in the United States.

X. CONCLUSION ⋮

THE PERSONAL OBSERVATIONS, judgments and concepts that have formed the contents of this book have been accumulated in the course of my forty-year career as a professional actor. I have been blessed by my experiences in the acting business, and I am grateful for the opportunities I've been given to pass on what I have learned.

All the examples I have cited and the conclusions I have drawn from them reflect my own taste and sensibilities. I hope that no actor or director or writer whose work I have referenced will be offended by what I have written. I have done my best to avoid negative critical evaluations, except in those instances in which some important point could not have been better illustrated by another example.

Throughout this book, I have made note of Academy Awards won by actors, directors, writers and others, but I have not given similar treatment to winners of Tonys and Emmys. The distinction has nothing to do with my opinion of the relative value of one award over another, but rather is based on the accessibility of the referenced work. Theatrical motion pictures, because of their availability on tape and DVD, provide a permanent, historical record. I have offered as many of these as seemed relevant in support or illustration of the ideas being presented. I trust that readers unfamiliar with the referenced material will take advantage (selectively, to be sure) of its availability.

I recognize that some of what is contained herein uses a vocabulary that actors might not be used to, because my terminology doesn't match the traditional forms. Wherever my expressions and descriptions have differed from more commonly used terms, it is only because I have observed that the popularly accepted words and explanations are more confusing than clarifying and that a direct and uncomplicated approach is better. Having been exposed to my ideas throughout the content of this book, the majority of readers will, I hope, agree.

It seems to me that for any actor, the only validity of a teacher's work is in the actor's ability to use that teacher's ideas to become a successful practitioner of the craft. That is my goal as a teacher and that has been the goal of this book. If *Acting and How to Be Good at It* empowers actors to be better and more confident craftsmen (and artists) and if non-actors become better informed audiences and critics, then I will have succeeded. To those ends, I have done my best.

ACKNOWLEDGEMENTS

THE EVENTS IN MY LIFE which contributed to the contents of this book were many and varied, and I need to acknowledge as many people as I can recall whose friendship, generosity, guidance, encouragement, patience or love, which were often translated into important jobs, brought me to this point.

To begin with, I thank everyone I've worked with whose names I have mentioned in the text of this volume for the important positive impressions they made on me that caused me to write about the experiences. Some of those whom I have already credited in my first book will be acknowledged again here because their effects upon me were so important, however brief those particular moments might have been. Unfortunately, many of these people have passed on, and others were just not appropriately thanked when an expression of gratitude would have been timely. I deeply regret that I missed those opportunities. Nevertheless, I will thank all of them here and now.

First is the unconditional love and everything that came with it that I received from my parents, Beulah and Dave. The only-child praise and adulation that they heaped upon me, frequently undeservedly, were an immeasurable emotional support whenever I needed it. I recognize that some of my less desirable traits might also have resulted from their unbridled affection. However, I (and those around me) have benefited from the gradual process of working some of that out of myself.

While in my sophomore year at Tulane University's Freeman School of Business, two friends who were students at Newcomb College (the women's part of Tulane), Duane Raffie and Paula Ross, both from New Orleans, convinced me (with the enticing prospect of meeting "a lot of girls") to audition for an original musical play. That theatrical experience (my first) prompted my decision to be an actor (Duane and Paula subsequently married two high school friends of mine; and Joel and Duane Zimmerman and Harvey and Paula Hoffman are still married, and we are still friends). Monroe Lippman, Chairman of Tulane's Theatre Department, and Danny Mullin, who taught the only acting course I took in college, provided me with an important introduction to theatre. Michael Parver, an M.F.A. candidate who directed me in that first play and three others (and who became my roommate in New York, helping to make my relocation financially possible), was another encouraging influence at that critical point in my life. I am indebted to all the foregoing for their seminal influence on my decision to embark on this career path.

Before my graduation from Tulane, another student, Jackie Marx, introduced me to Edward Gschwind, a regional auditioner for the American Academy of Dramatic Arts in New York. That meeting, my audition, and Mr. Gschwind's recommendation gave me a somewhat effortless (or so I thought at the time) entrée into the mysterious world of New York show business. I am grateful to both of them. I am also grateful to Frances Fuller, then president of the American Academy, for her acceptance and for the scholarship I received later that enabled me to continue in the second year.

One month before my classes at the American Academy were scheduled to begin, I was hired by Morris Goldstein, managing partner at Francis I. DuPont & Company at One Wall Street, to work as a statistical assistant from 6:00 P.M. to 2:00 A.M. five nights a week. That job and my subsequent employer (and friend) John Doherty, at Blyth Eastman Dillon, financed six years of actor training and career struggles that preceded my viability as a professional. I am very grateful.

Of all my teachers in New York, only Clifford Jackson appeared to hold out any hope for my success as an actor, and I thank him for the years of very patient acting and singing lessons he gave me (at a deep volume discount from his regular fees, because my gross inability to carry a tune required a lot of work from both of us). By the time I got around to calling his home in New York to thank him for all that he meant to my success, Clifford Jackson had already died. Neglecting to acknowledge his encouragement and kindness in a timely manner was a personal failing of mine that I deeply, deeply regret.

Pat and Fred Carmichael hired me for my first professional (but non-Equity) summer acting job after the American Academy, and they stuck with me despite an unexpected, intrusive personal incident during our rehearsal period over which I had no control, but which temporarily disrupted the harmony of the rehearsal process nonetheless. I was fortunate for the assistance provided to me at that time in that situation by my friend Howard Fallis in Houston. The following year, an acting classmate, Patricia Frawley, introduced me to her friend Bill Howe, who recommended me to Jack and Ana Edler Brown (who became my friends), which led to the acquisition of my Equity card in a season of stock they produced in Irwin, Pennsylvania. Without the validation I received from those early experiences, my career might have been stopped before it started. I am grateful.

I also want to acknowledge my gratitude to the New York agents who, at various times, provided important help when I needed it. Jay Jacobs, at the William Morris Agency, was the first agent I ever met, and his assistance and friendship over many years in New York and Los Angeles were very important to my self-esteem, in addition to the jobs that resulted from the relationship.

Ruth Webb is the first agent through whom I ever got a job, in a summer stock season in Cooperstown, New York. Gus Schirmer was my agent for the first musical job I ever did in an important theatre, *South Pacific* at Jones Beach (New York Production Contract), directed by William Hammerstein, whose father Oscar Hammerstein (with Richard Rodgers) had written the play. Later, John Sekura, at

AFA (which later became ICM), represented me when I worked for producer Robert Ludlum (who became a renowned, best-selling writer of spy novels).

Of the few agents who were receptive to my first attempts to get television commercials, Beth Allen, at the Michael Hartig Agency, was the most aggressive on my behalf, and my first commercial (for Barney's men's store in New York) came through her efforts. Lester Lewis was my first signed commercial agent. Fifi Oscard was my last exclusive New York agent, and her introductions to agents in Hollywood paved the way for my successful transition to California. Estelle Tepper, an agent in Fifi's office (and later a very successful casting director in New York and Hollywood), submitted me to Sally Dennison, Carlo Ponti's New York casting director, which resulted in my first movie role (in *Lady Liberty*).

I am grateful to all of them and to the many agents, casting directors, producers, and directors in New York who were so supportive and who facilitated my transformation from fearful beginner to successful professional.

I especially want to mention three directors, Arnie Freeman, Steven Keats and George C. Scott, for the personal thank you notes they sent me for *auditioning*, even though they didn't hire me. Being actors, they must have known how important those notes would be.

After I had done my first commercial, an actress friend, Natalie Helms, asked if I would take the Weist-Barron School's commercial course with her. That class was followed by my employment over the next few years in hundreds of commercials.

Dwight Weist and Bob Barron subsequently asked me to participate in their first soap opera course at a time when all but two of those shows were produced in New York. The producers and casting directors I met during that course led to a lot of work. Most important was my introduction to casting director Joan D'Incecco, resulting in two years of recurring work as Walter Witherspoon on ABC's *One Life to Live*. That show's producer, Doris Quinlan, later hired me for an excellent television movie role in Hollywood. The foregoing sequence of events was instrumental in the course of my career, and those who precipitated those events have my undying gratitude.

I would be remiss if I didn't acknowledge the information offered to me by some of my acting colleagues (and friends) in New York who had already worked in Hollywood. I particularly want to thank Darrell Zwerling, Jay Gerber and Jack Aaron for their help and encouragement preceding my first trip west.

I also thank Jim Raymond, a Hollywood-based actor whom I had met in New York when we worked together in a commercial for Equitable Life, for his generous personal and professional kindnesses on my behalf during my first months in Los Angeles.

From the very beginning of my career in Hollywood, there were a few agents who were helpful, even though they wouldn't represent me. I especially appreciate the advice given me by Susan Smith, whom I had known previously as a casting director in New York, and the time that Larry Masser, then at the Mishkin Agency, generously gave me in a very informative meeting. Phil Volman, at the Contemporary-Korman Agency, who sent me to my first network television pilot audition (before he became my agent at Beakel-Jennings) and Kevin Casselman were also encouraging (in what I eventually came to understand as a uniquely Hollywood way of gentle non-rejection rejection). I am grateful for the confidence that I was, nonetheless, able to take from my meetings with them in my first week in Los Angeles.

My most successful meetings in my first week or so in Hollywood were with television commercial agents, all of whom wanted to represent me. I'm grateful to Charles Stern and Herb Tannen for their interest and to Don Pitts (who later became my voice agent) and Leanna Levy whose early interest and friendship finally resulted in her becoming my current voice agent. The longest agent relationship I ever had (which continues to this day) began with the Jack Wormser Agency, where Jack, Roger Heldfond and Sandy Joseph became my first commercial agents. I signed with that agency primarily because of Sandy's interest and urging (Sandy, always an excellent student of the business, later became a successful personal manager; her insights have proven valuable and lasting to me).

I am grateful for the business relationship that has progressed through many name changes and many agents, including Brian Rix, who was instrumental in my acquisition of a theatrical (film and television) agent at a time when I needed that representation, Cindy Kazarian, Pamm Spencer, Alicia Ruskin, Pat Brady and Brooke Nuttall. Joan Green, who had been at the agency, has become one of the most prominent personal managers in the business, and Joan has generously given me her time and advice over the years whenever I ask. My years with the Jack Wormser Agency (and its successors) have made important contributions to my life and career.

During the six months that it took me to find my first theatrical agent in Los Angeles, casting directors became my best career support. Joel Thurm, who had offered me a part several years earlier in New York (which I turned down for what ultimately proved to be very good career considerations) when he worked for the legendary Broadway producer David Merrick, provided my first television audition in Hollywood (for *Newhart*), and he introduced me to the other casting directors at CBS Studio Center. Joel's encouragement and the events resulting from that audition (which I didn't win) were critical to my good start (five television episodes, two television movies and a feature movie for Peter Bogdanovich) in that first half year. Of the forty-four casting directors whom I have already acknowledged (in my earlier volume), I need to again specifically thank Pam Dixon (who recommended me to Joan Scott, founder of Writers & Artists Agency, and Arnold Rifkin, who later became president of William Morris) and Reuben Cannon (who introduced me to the Gersh Agency) for taking the extra effort to recommend me to those important agents (who declined to represent me, although Joan Scott did become my agent one year later). I also need to extend my appreciation to Judy Elkins, who has been so helpful to me on many occasions when I needed the benefit of her casting expertise.

The most important casting director relationship I had was with Tom Jennings, then at Warner Brothers (casting *Kung Fu*, among other series). Tom's introduction to manager-attorney Hurley Graffius resulted in my first theatrical representation in Hollywood (as part of Hurley's small and distinguished client roster that included only Lee Van Cleef, John Ireland, Cesar Romero, Burl Ives, Raf Vallone, Joseph Cotten and me). Casting directors began to know me as the new actor in town who doesn't have an agent but has an important lawyer.

After I had been working (through Hurley) in Los Angeles for about six months, Alex Brewis became my first theatrical agent thanks to a generous introduction and recommendation from his client, the excellent, distinguished character actor M. Emmet Walsh, whom I had known since my acting student days in New York. I am grateful to both of those men for their part in my career development in that important year.

Tom Jennings ultimately became my agent, and our association lasted through three separate agency changes including his partnership with Walter Beakel, who also represented me well during that period, as did Bernie Carneol, at Progressive Artists Agency, for whose representation I am very appreciative. I am grateful for the contributions Tom, Hurley and Walter made in establishing me as a respectable commodity in Hollywood. It was Tom's arrangement of a meeting for me with casting director Alan Shayne (who, fortunately and surprisingly to me, actually recalled an earlier meeting that we had in New York) that led directly to the single most important (because of its impact on the entire course of my career) job I ever had, in *All the President's Men*. I could never thank Alan enough for what that job has meant to me.

I also owe a debt of gratitude to personal manager Philip Gittelman for the important recommendations he made for me. I especially thank Michael Belson and Eric Klass for their high-class representation. It was a privilege to be part of their strictly limited forty-five-client roster. Agents Michael Zanuck, Dale Garrick, Rosemary Edwards, Emily Hope, Mitchell Kaplan and Bob Gersh have offered uncommon help to me in many ways unconnected to any personal representation (although Mitchell and Michael were my agents, briefly), and I am grateful.

Of the stage directors for whom I have worked in Hollywood, I am especially appreciative of the interesting opportunities created for me by the efforts of Park Perrine, Robert Scheerer, Allan Miller and John Schuck (Allan and John are both excellent actors, as well). And I am grateful for the work of playwrights William Blinn and Martin E. Brooks (also an excellent actor), for a variety of reasons.

Film directors, more than any other category of professionals in the business, are responsible for my career progression, longevity and any positive reputation that I may have acquired along the way. Those I have worked for comprise a distinguished list, and I am grateful for my association with all of them. In some cases, I have received important (to me) acknowledgements and favors which were directly connected to my work in their films, but sometimes those courtesies concerned other matters which demanded some extra effort on their part. In this regard, I want to mention Peter Medak, Delbert Mann, Richard Benjamin, Sydney Pollack, Alan J. Pakula, and Robert Redford (and Woody Allen, for whom I haven't yet worked, but who, nonetheless, extended an unexpected courtesy to me). Robert Redford, in particular, has been so generous to me that I can trace every important development in my career since 1975 either directly or indirectly to my association with him.

I am grateful to Redd Foxx, who requested me for his ABC television pilot, *My Buddy* (in which I had the odd, good fortune to play opposite Pamela Mason), and to Loretta Swit, who asked for me in a television movie (for which I wasn't hired). And I especially want to express my gratitude to the great television writer (and friend)

Robert W. Lensky, who wrote parts for me in two *Hallmark Hall of Fame* movies (even though neither of the directors hired me).

I have always been surprised and moved by letters of gratitude sent to me by people whose brief professional association with me was much more valuable to me than to them. It was I, not they, who should have done the thanking. I will take this opportunity to thank Robert Young, Bernie Orenstein, Saul Turteltaub, Douglas Cramer, Ross Hunter, Jacques Mapes and Gordon Davidson.

My teaching experience at the Academie Libanaise des Beaux-Arts (ALBA) in Beirut, Lebanon, in 2002, was one of the most rewarding professional experiences of my life. I am grateful to my friend Habib Fadel for making it possible, to Khalil Smayra for his friendship and his courage in entrusting his cinema students to me and, finally, to Georges Haddad, Director of ALBA, for his generosity and hospitality during my time in Lebanon.

I am fortunate and grateful for my friendship with Joe and Rachel Purcell, specifically for their contributions to my career in various ways. Joe, who is a skilled, multi-talented director, edited my first professional demo reel and, later, with Rachel, created a story on which we collaborated for a screenplay (and which Joe continually urged me to make better). I believe that their encouragement had a positive, lasting effect on my writing ability, such as it is.

My friend Merrilu Gordon also contributed to the development of whatever writing skills I now possess. She was responsible for a commission I received from The Heritage Foundation for a biography (which couldn't be completed because our friend and the subject of the project, the great political financier Henry Salvatori, died before I was able to get critical personal information).

I am also indebted to Sandy Climan, who, as an executive at CAA, graciously recommended my first screenplay to Catherine Tarr, an excellent writers agent in his agency. Cathy's patient guidance through several rewrites was instrumental in restructuring the work into a more commercial form. She worked very hard to market it.

Even though that script remains unsold, I am grateful to Cathy for her considerable efforts. What I learned from that experience about writing and the business of writing has been very helpful.

I am grateful to K Callan, who has been more than a good friend for a long time, for the inspiration I have gotten from the uncompromising truthfulness of her acting and from the sharing of her unflagging interest in the acting process. She has been an important personal and professional influence in my life in many ways.

Roger Karshner, a writer and publisher who has been my closest friend for many years, was responsible for my writing my first book, *Cold Reading and How to Be Good at It*. He suggested the subject, commissioned the book and published it. Without his friendship and encouragement, and the success of that book, this current volume would not have been written. Brad Lemack, my longtime manager and friend, also a publisher, subsequently asked me if I had another book in me. *Acting and How to Be Good at It* is that book.

I was fortunate to have been the recipient of their suggestions at the perfectly practical moments for me to embark on those writing projects, and I was equally fortunate that, having made the suggestions, they both had the ability and the intention to actually publish the books. I am grateful to Roger for the friendship and for all the good that has come from it. I am grateful to Brad for his friendship, his loyalty and his good advice.

I owe my life to God. I cannot recount the endless miracles of love, health and career that have been demonstrated in my life on a daily basis. I am eternally grateful beyond my ability to express it.

AFTRA, 171

aftra.com, 171

Academie Libanaise des Beaux-Arts, xix

Academy of Motion Picture Arts and

Sciences, 158, 171

Academy of Television Arts and Sciences, 171

Academy Players Directory, 172

Accent, 27, 29, 71, 113-115

Accents, 27, 28, 72, 115

Acting and real life, 9, 10, 37, 58, 64

Acting business, 2, 21, 102, 119, 161, 162,

Acting Business and How to be Good at It, The, 161

Acting coach, 27

Acting exercises, 85

Acting schools, 101

Acting teachers, 101

Acting, acquired attributes, 162

Acting, art of, 9

Acting, career attributes, 19

Acting, craft of, 1-3, 9, 10, 13, 20, 24, 26, 31, 32, 34, 85, 101, 106, 107, 162, 165, 174

Acting, film, 11, 12, 22

Acting, professional, 3, 5, 21, 23, 101, 165

Acting, slick, 12, 13

Acting, stage, 11, 12, 22,

Acting, what is, 8

Actor and writer, 109

Actors Equity Association, 171

actorsequity.org, 171

Actor's conceit, 103

Actor's essence, 45

Actors, star, 7, 28, 127, 156, 166

Adjustments, truthful, 7, 56

A.D.R., 153

Adventures in the Screen Trade, 167

Agenting, 23

Agents, 158, 164-166

Agents, commercial, 157

ALBA, xix

Alice Miller, 129

All in the Family, 169

All That Jazz, 147

All the President's Men, 26, 93, 110, 130, 152, 169

Allen, Woody, 18, 29, 121

American Academy of Dramatic Arts, 26, 89, 102, 167

American Film Institute, 131, 168, 171

American Film Institute Desk Reference, 171

Amplified Realism, 10, 11, 18, 79

Anderson, Dame Judith, 72

Andrews, Dana, 13

Anheuser Busch Natural Light Beer, 150

Annie Hall, 29

Another Conversation, xvii, xix

Apartment, The, 132

APPROACHES TO TRAINING, 31

Arc, 85

Arnold, Danny, 154

Art of acting, 9

Arthur, 11

As Good As It Gets, 136

At Long Last Love, 118

At-oneness, 16, 17

Attitude, 101, 117, 118, 155, 156, 161

Attitude and essence, 47

Audition, 1, 16, 25, 46, 48, 56, 85, 103, 105, 107, 108, 112, 113, 120, 127, 128, 133, 143, 144, 157-159, 172

Audition, rehearsal, and performance acting, 15, 16, 27, 33

Auditioning, 1, 48, 103, 144

Auditions, 33, 105, 156, 157, 165, 169, 172

Automated dialogue replacement, 153

Bacon, Kevin, 83

Back Stage, 170

Back Stage West, 170

Balsam. Martin, 111

Barney Miller, 120

Barrymore, John, 72

Basil Hoffman School of Acting, 25

Beat, 75, 76, 122

Beats, 76, 122

Beautiful Mind, A, 114, 133

Behavior, 6, 7, 9-12, 17, 31-34, 37, 38, 42-44, 46, 49, 51, 53-58, 62, 64, 65, 67, 76, 78-80, 82, 84, 85, 87, 88, 94, 108, 112, 117, 118, 121-124, 130, 134, 135, 142, 149

Behavior, natural sequence of, 53, 54

Behavior, programmed, 56, 78, 79

Being There, 71

Ben-Hur, 131, 132

Benjamin, Richard, 8, 95, 129, 135

Benjy Stone, 129

Bennett, Robert, 93

Best Years of our Lives, The, 15, 131

Bestor, Rollie, 156

Bicycle Thief, The, 15

Big Deal on Madonna Street, 136

Blazing Saddles, 135

Blinn, William, 113

Bloody Mary, 20

Bogdanovich, Peter, 118

Bologna, Joseph, 7

Borgnine, Ernest, 17

Bound for Glory, 150

Boys Don't Cry, 17

Boys Town, 114

Brando, Marlon, 46, 70, 75, 80

Brazilian play, 89

Break down a script, 121, 123

Brian's Song, 113

Bridge on the River Kwai, The, 17

Bridget Jones's Diary, 114

Bring it down, 136

Broadway, 12, 21, 26, 72, 133, 163, 166

Brooks, Mel, 95, 135

Brooks, Richard, 121

Brown, Jack, 89

Brynner, Yul, 114

Bugsy, 147

Business of Acting, The, 171

Business plan, 163, 166

Business tools, 163

Butch Cassidy and the Sundance Kid, 111

"Button, Button," 135

Cabaret, 125

Caesar, Sid, 62

Cage, Nicolas, 82

Cagney, James, 70

Caine, Michael, 28

Callan, K, 171, 172

Cannon, Reuben, 169, 170

Cape Fear, 17

Captain Landry, 90

Captains Courageous, 114

CAREER MANAGEMENT, 161

Career management, 2

Career mistakes, 164

Carter, Helena Bonham, 29

Casablanca, 114

Casting, 105, 115, 127, 128, 156, 157, 159, 170, 172

Casting, commercial, 156-159

Casting Director Guide, 172

Casting directors, 23, 25, 27, 28, 46, 105, 164, 166, 168-170, 172

Character essence, 105

CHARACTER STUDY, 37

Character study, 32, 56

Charley Malloy, 75

Chekhov, Anton, 18, 33

Charly, 71

Cider House Rules, The, 28

Cinematographer, 14, 129, 146, 150, 151, 168

Citizen Kane, 152

Classical acting, 16, 72

Clooney, George, 52

Close Encounters of the Third Kind, 93, 120

Clouds Over Europe, 152

Coach, acting, 27, 31, 38, 85, 138, 139, 149, 165

Coach, dialect and speech, 72, 113

Coal Miner's Daughter, 28

Cobb, Lee J., 17

Coburn, Charles, 164

Cold Reading and How to be Good at It, 1

Collaborative cooperation, 145

Columbo, 68, 69, 119, 148

Comedy, 18

Comes a Horseman, 42, 56, 130, 148

Comfort zone, 57

Coming Home, 104

Commercial agents, 157

Commercial auditions, 157

Commercial casting, 156, 157

COMMERCIALS, 157

Commodore Roseabove, 91

Communion, 65

Company, 133

Compass, 85

CONCLUSION, 173

Conflict, 45, 78

Conflicts, 45, 78, 112, 121

Conservatories, 101

Conversation, A, xvii, xix

Cooperstown, New York, 90

Coppola, Francis Ford, 46

Coppola, Sofia, 140

Cornerstones of Truth, 16, 112

Coster, Nicolas, 121

Costume, 147

Costumers, 147

Costumes, 145

Craft of acting, 2, 9, 85, 162

Creative decisions in movies, 141

Creative decisions in television, 141

Creative decisions in theatre, 140

Crosby, Norm, 62

Crowe, Russell, 29

Cues, inner, 32, 50, 51

Cues, light, 43

Cues, sound, 43

Cukor, George, 167

Dahlberg, Kenneth, 93

Daily Variety, 168, 170

Dangerous, 136

Danson, Ted, 98

Davis, Bette, 136, 166

Davis, Brad, 135

Day-Lewis, Daniel, 17

DECISIONS ON TRAINING, 21

Deer Hunter, The, 8, 65

Demonstrating, 54, 55, 58, 81, 82

DeNiro, Robert, 28

DeSica, Vittorio, 15

DeSalvo, Anne, 7, 129

Dialect coach, 72, 113

Dialects, 27-29, 31, 71, 72, 113, 114

Director of photography (DP), 150

Director, film, 133

Director, stage, 72, 140

Director, television, 141, 142

Discovery, 11, 12, 37, 42, 58, 107-109, 121, 143

Doctor Zhivago, 115

DOING THE JOB, 117

Donen, Stanley, 125

Double O Kid, The, 96

Double-talk, 62

Douglas, Kirk, 136

Down with Love, 127

Dr. Hawk, 89

Dr. Jekyll and Mr. Hyde, 114

Dramatic purpose, 82

Drollhauser, 133

Dubbing, 153

Duke's Oak Theatre, 90

Durning, Charles, 167

Duvall, Robert, 114

Eddie Fuselli, 92

Edwards, Blake, 126

Electric Horseman, The, 121, 126, 131, 144, 149, 150

Elias, Alix, 168

emmys.com, 171

Emotional stimuli, 58

Energize the script, 121-123

Episodic television, 120, 126, 142

Equity card, 89

Essence and attitude, 47

Essence, character, 44-47, 105

Evans, Maurice, 72, 73

Exercises, acting, 85

Fadel, Habib, xix

Falk, Peter, 69, 119

Fay Compton School of Acting, 166

Feelings, xix, 14, 17, 24, 25, 32-35, 37, 40-43, 47, 51, 57-59, 61, 62, 64-67, 73, 76, 81, 84, 86, 88, 99, 100, 103, 108, 112, 121-124, 127, 135, 159

Film acting, 11, 12, 22

Film editing, 145

Film editor, 151

Film Encyclopedia, The, 171

Fonda, Henry, 156

Fonda, Jane, 57, 104, 121, 149

Force, Joan, 90

Fordham University, 89

Forrest Gump, 71

Foxx, Redd, 169, 170

Freeman, Morgan, 17

French Connection, The, 125

French Kiss, 114

Friedman, Kim, 168

Froehlich, Marcy, 147

From Here to Eternity, 17

Fugitive, The, 28

Fuller, Frances, 102

Furth, George, 133

Gandhi, 17

Garrett, Hank, 96

Gertz, Jami, 168

Ghelderode, Michel de, 34

Gielgud, Sir John, 11, 12, 72

Goals, long-term, 21, 163, 164

Goals, short-term, 20, 163

Goals, training, 20, 21

Godfather, The, 46

Godfather: Part II, The, 28

Golden Boy, 92

Goldman, William, 111, 167

Gone With the Wind, 12

Goodfellas, 28

Grant, Cary, 28

Great Expectations, 150

Green, Adolph, 7

Green, Guy, 150, 168

Greenberg, Robbie, 150

Greenstreet, Sidney, 164

Grizzard, George, 57

Grouping, 74, 75

Gruskoff, Michael, 95, 135

Guidelines, career, 163

Guinness, Sir Alec, 17, 166

Guthrie, Sir Tyrone, 72

Hackman, Gene, 125

Halliwell's Film Guide, 171

Halliwell's Who's Who in the
   Movies, 171

Hamlet, 16, 71, 72, 148

Hanks, Tom, 71

Hannah and Her Sisters, 28

Harden, Marcia Gay, 83

Hauer, Rutger, 28

Hepburn, Audrey, 84

Herb Lee, 129, 135

Heston, Charlton, 132

Hoffman, Dustin, 71, 131

Hollywood Reporter, The,
   168, 170

Holocaust, 115

Homework, 2, 12, 14-16, 31-
   33, 37, 57, 58, 105-108,
   117, 124, 127, 128, 132,
   143, 144, 147

House of Sand and Fog, 114

Houseman, John, 26

Howard, Ron, 94, 133

Hunchback of Notre Dame, The, 152

Hunt, Martita, 166

Hunter, Holly, 28, 106

Hustler, The, 130

Hutton, Timothy, 111

Ibsen, Henrik, 33

Ichabod, 89

Imagination, 17, 37, 121

imdb.com, 171

Immediate purpose, 82

Improvisation, 15, 33

In the Heat of the Night, 28

Indicating, 54, 137

Inner cues, 32, 50, 51

Internet, 24, 170-172

Internet Movie Database, 171

Interviews, commercials, 175, 176

INTRODUCTION, 1

Ivanov, 12

Jeffersons, The, 169

Jennifer: A Woman's Story, 150, 168

Jennings, Tom, 168

Jezebel, 136

Johnny Belinda, 106

Jones Beach, 11

Jones, Tommy Lee, 28

Joseph, Sandy, 169

Judging acting schools, 22

Juilliard, 26

Julia, 26, 111

Katz, Ephraim, 171

Kaye, Danny, 64

Kazan, Elia, 75

Keaton, Michael, 94

Kennedy family, 71

KGB, 97

Killing Fields, The, 15

King and I, The, 114

King, Perry, 26

Kingsley, Sir Ben, 17, 114

Kline, Kevin, 114

Klute, 104

Kramer vs. Kramer, 131, 149

L.A.Confidential, 29

Lady Liberty, 136, 140

Last King of Scotland, The, 17

Laura, 13

Law, Jude, 147

Le Gallienne, Eva, 166

Lear, Norman, 169, 170

Leaving Las Vegas, 82, 83

Leigh, Vivien, 12

Lemack, Brad, 171

Lemmon, Jack, 132

Let Him Have It, 135

Life purpose, 81

Light cues, 43

Lighting, 145, 146
Line reading, 84, 138, 139
Linn-Baker, Mark, 7, 95, 129
Listening, 22, 84, 106, 107
Little Mary Sunshine, 90
Longly, 93
Looping, 140, 153
Lorca, Federico Garcia, 33
Loren, Sophia, 136
Los Angeles Times, The, 130
Lost in Translation, 140
Lost Weekend, The, 132
Lucey, Paul, 109
Luck, 6, 20, 167, 169
Lucky Lady, 125, 135
Lust for Life, 114

MacLaine,Shirley, 26
Macy, Bill, 7, 129
Maggiorani, Lamberto, 15
Makeup, 126, 128, 145, 146,
    151, 152
Management, career, 161
Managers, 23, 164-166
Managing, 23
Marathon Man, 149
Marble Arch Productions, 168
M*A*S*H, 119
McLachlan, Duncan, 96
Medak, Peter, 98, 134
Melvin and Howard, 98
Mendocino, California, 98
Melman, Jeff, 154

Memorizing, 31, 73, 88, 107,
    123, 124, 126, 127
Memory of emotion, 57
Milagro Beanfield War, The,
    65, 96, 150
Million Dollar Baby, 17
Mills, Sir John, 17
Minnelli, Liza, 125
Mistakes, hiring, 145
Mitchum, Robert, 17
Moment, 9-12, 16, 41, 51, 52,
    54-59, 65-70, 75, 76, 79, 80,
    82-85, 88, 89, 92, 93, 104,
    106, 111-113, 117, 118, 122,
    123, 125-129, 133, 139, 140,
    143, 149, 152, 159
Moment, living in the, 48
Moneychangers, The, 119
Monicelli, Mario, 136, 140
Monologue power, 33
Monster, 17
Montgomery, Elizabeth, 150
More the Merrier, The, 164
Morgan, Harry, 119
Moscow, 63, 97, 144
Mr. Roberts, 132
Mrs. Miniver, 131
Murray, Bill, 140
Music of the Heart, 149
Musical theatre, 21
My Buddy, 170
My Fair Lady, 167
My Favorite Year, 7, 95,
    129, 135

My Left Foot, 17
Mystic River, 82, 83

Nantucket, 91
Narrative, 43, 59, 109, 110
Naturalism, 80
Nelson, Tracy, 168
Ngor, Haing S., 15
Nicholson, Jack, 136
Night Court, 120
Night Shift, 94, 133
Nolte, Nick, 149
Now Casting, 172
nowcasting.com, 172

Objective, 38, 40, 54, 80, 81, 84
Obstacles, 19, 45, 76-78, 104, 121
Obie, 89
Oedepus Rex, 115
Off-off-Broadway, 89
Oh Dad, Poor Dad, Mama's Hung You in the Closet and I'm Feelin' So Sad, 89
Old Gringo, 104
Oldsmobile, 150
Olivier, Sir Laurence (Lord), 71, 72, 148, 156
O'Meara, Tim, 152
On Golden Pond, 156
On the Waterfront, 17, 46, 75
One Flew Over the Cuckoo's Nest, 136

One Life to Live, 168
Ordinary People, 94, 111, 119
Organizer, The, 136
oscars.org, 171
Othello, 71
O'Toole, Peter, 7, 95, 136
Out of Africa, 131
Out of Sight, 52
Over the top, 136

Pacino, Al, 28, 136
Pakula, Alan J., 56, 93, 110, 130, 148, 168, 169
Paper Chase, The, 26
Park Place, 120
Parker, Sarah Jessica, 168
Pasadena, 98
Patton, 130
Peck, Gregory, 8, 104
Pembroke Lodge, 166
Penn, Sean, 82
Permission, 55
Petticoat Fever, 90
Photographer, 149, 158, 163, 166
Phrasing, 73, 74, 127
Physicality, 29, 43, 47, 48, 150
Piano, The, 28, 106
Pittsburgh, 89
Playwright, 86, 103, 110, 125, 146
Plummer, Christopher, 119
Point of a line, 65, 66

Pollack, Sydney, 126, 131, 144, 150

Pollock, 83

Portobello Circus, The, 89

Possession of Joel Delaney, The, 26

Preminger, Otto, 130

Prestone II, 150

Principal Dingleman, 168

Privileged information, xvii, 51, 52

PROFESSIONAL ACTING, 5

Professional acting, 1-3, 5, 21, 23, 101, 165

Professional school, 101

Professionalism, 5-8, 16, 102, 117, 118, 128, 152, 165

Programmed behavior, 56, 78

Pronunciation, 70

Props, 86, 123, 126, 128, 145, 146, 148, 149, 152

Pulse, 122

Purpose, 10, 49, 78, 81, 82, 83, 88, 108, 112, 119, 121, 159

Purpose, dramatic, 82

Purpose, immediate, 82

Purpose, life, 81

Quinlan, Doris, 168

Quinn, Anthony, 114

Rain Man, 71, 131

Rains, Claude, 114

Rasbury, Andy, 90

Raymond Poole, 113

Reagan, Ronald, 27

Redeker, Quinn, 8

Redford, Robert, 93, 94, 96, 110, 111, 121, 131, 149, 150, 169

Rehearsal, 11-16, 27, 32, 33, 57, 58, 106-108, 110, 124-126, 129, 143, 145, 149

Repertory, 21, 91, 163, 166

Reporting, 38, 83, 84

Reynolds, Burt, 118, 125

Richardson, Sir Ralph, 152

Road to Perdition, 147

Robards, Jason, 26, 42, 57, 111

Robertson, Cliff, 71

Robbins, Tim, 83

Roizman, Owen, 150

Romeo and Juliet, 115

Roots, 113

Roth, Tim, 29

Rudley, Herbert, 72

Ruling Class, The, 135

Rush, Geoffrey, 17

Russell, Harold, 15

Ryan's Daughter, 17

sag.org, 171

Sacharow, Lawrence, 89

Samson, Barry, 144

Sanford and Son, 169, 170

Sargent, Alvin, 111

Sartre, Jean-Paul, 34

Save the Tiger, 132

Saving Private Ryan, 120

Saxon, John, 121

Scene study, 32, 108

Scenery, 145, 149

Scent of a Woman, 28

Schindler's List, 120

Schools, acting, 101

Scott, George C., 130, 136

Screen Actors Guild, 158, 171

Screenwriter and the Actor, The, 109

Scripts, complete, 159

Scripts, incomplete, 120

Secret Life of Walter Mitty, The, 64

Sexy Beast, 17

Sellers, Peter, 71

Serenading Louie, 131

Shakespeare, William, 16, 25, 72

Shayne, Alan, 168

Shine, 17

Shot at Glory, A, 114

Showcases, 23, 166

Sikking, James, 121

Simon, Neil, 18, 135

Simpson, John, 131

Slate, 159

Slick acting, 12, 13

Smayra, Khalil, xix

Sneller, Jeffrey, 144

Soldier of Orange, 28

Soap operas, 21, 22

Sound cues, 43

Sound effects, 145

Sound mixer, 129

Sound of Music, The, 152

Sourcetext, 65

South Pacific, 11, 20

Soviet Union, 97, 144

Spacek, Sissy, 28

Speech coach, 113

Spielberg, Steven, 93, 120

Square Pegs, 168, 170

Stage acting, 11, 12, 22

Stage directions, 43

Stage production, 140, 145

Stanley Inchbeck, 119

Star actors, 7, 28, 127, 156, 166

Steenburgen, Mary, 98

Steiger, Rod, 28, 75

Steinberg, Norman, 95, 135

Stewart, Bob, 172

Straight Wharf Theatre, 91

Stratford, Connecticut Shakespeare Festival, 25

Streep, Meryl, 114, 149,

Street Smart, 17

Streetcar Named Desire, A, 12

Strindberg, August, 34

Subjective Situation Perception, 16, 38-40, 42-44, 61, 66, 86, 108, 121, 123, 138

Subtext, 45, 64, 65, 88

Surprise, 13, 56-58, 74, 78, 132, 143

Sutherland, Donald, 94, 119

Swank, Hilary, 17

Switch, 126

Sy Benson, 129

TABLE OF CONTENTS, ix

Teachers, acting, 1, 22, 23, 101

Teachers, destructive, 24

Television director, 141, 142

Tempo, 71, 122

Ten from "Your Show of Shows", 62

Tender Mercies, 114

Terms of Endearment, 26, 136

Terry Malloy, 75

Theron, Charlize, 17

Thought pause, 67-69

Thought reading, 139

Thousand Clowns, A, 111

To Kill a Mockingbird, 8

Tone of the script, 79, 80, 106, 111, 119, 146

Tootsie, 131

Tory, The, 89

Tracy, Spencer, 114

Training, necessity of, 20

Trent, Sybil, 156

Truths, fundamental, 103

Tunes of Glory, 17

Twilight Zone, The, 135

Two Women, 136

Typecasting, 105

U.S. Senate Government Affairs Committee, 38

Ultimate Warrior, The, 114

Under Fire, 149

Vanzina, Carlo, 140

Verbal punctuation, 73

Vito Corleone, 46

Viva Zapata, 114

Vocality, 70, 71

Wait Until Dark, 84

Walken, Christopher, 65, 96

Walking Peoria, 113

Walsh, M. Emmet, 96

Walter Mitty, 64

Warden, Jack, 111

Wardrobe, 123, 126, 128, 129, 142, 146-148, 152

Warner Brothers, 27, 168

Washington Post, 110

Webb, Clifton, 13

Webb, Ruth, 90

Weege, Reinhold, 120

West Side Story, 152

Weston, Jack, 84

Wexler, Haskell, 150

Wheeler, Curtis, 90

Whitaker, Forest, 17

White Barn Theatre, 89

Who's Afraid of Virginia Woolf, 150

Wilder, Billy, 132

Wildwood Enterprises, 110

Wilson, Lanford, 131

Winkler, Henry , 94

Winningham, Mare, 135

Wise, Robert, 152

Wolsky, Albert, 147

Wormser, Jack, 169

Wyler, William, 15, 131, 132

Wyman, Jane, 106

Yankee Doodle Dandy, 70

Yellow Feather, 90

Your Show of Shows, 62

Zampese, Alan, 89

Zellweger, Renee, 114, 127,

Zorba the Greek, 114